Merchants, Midwives, and
Laboring Women

Merchants, Midwives, and Laboring Women

Italian Migrants in Urban America

DIANE C. VECCHIO

UNIVERSITY OF ILLINOIS PRESS

Urbana and Chicago

© 2006 by Diane C. Vecchio
All rights reserved
∞ This book is printed on acid-free paper.
Manufactured in the United States of America

C 5 4 3 2 1

Library of Congress Cataloging-in-Publication Data
Vecchio, Diane C., 1949–
Merchants, midwives, and laboring women: Italian migrants in urban America /
Diane C. Vecchio.
    p.   cm. — (Statue of Liberty–Ellis Island Centennial series)
Includes bibliographical references and index.
ISBN-13: 978-0-252-03039-0 (alk. paper)
ISBN-10: 0-252-03039-7 (paper: alk. paper)
1. Italian American women—New York (State)—Endicott—
Economic conditions. 2. Italian American women—Wisconsin—
Milwaukee—Economic conditions. 3. Italian American women—
Employment—New York (State)—Endicott—History. 4. Italian American
women—Employment—Wisconsin—Milwaukee—History. 5. Alien labor—
New York (State)—Endicott—History. 6. Alien labor—Wisconsin—
Milwaukee—History. 7. Women employees—New York (State)—Endicott—
History. 8. Women employees—Wisconsin—Milwaukee—History. 9. Endicott
(N.Y.)—Economic conditions. 10. Milwaukee (Wis.)—Economic conditions.
I. Title. II. Series.
HD8081.18V43   2006
331.4'089'51073—dc22   2005018548

*I lovingly dedicate this work to the memory of
my grandmother, Rose Marie Julian (Giuliano) Verrico,
and my sister, Rosemarie Vecchio Terzo,
whose love and commitment to the family
will forever remain alive.*

Contents

Illustrations follow page 60

Acknowledgments

I OWE SPECIAL DEBTS of gratitude to many people who helped make this book possible. The efforts of Luciano Iorizzo, who salvaged the employment records of Endicott Johnson as the corporation began to fold in the 1970s, made it possible for me to re-create the working lives of Italian women. I would like to thank him and Gerald Zahavi for sharing Endicott Johnson records with me.

Much of my work on Milwaukee's Italians would have been impossible without the help of Mario Carini, a local historian of Italians in Milwaukee. For his insight into the Italian community, the numerous contacts he arranged for me, and the meals I shared with his sister and mother, I thank him.

I would like to thank Steve Daily of the Milwaukee County Historical Society for allowing me to quote from the interviews I conducted with Milwaukee's Italians that are now part of their archival collection. I appreciate, too, the cooperation of the Wisconsin State Historical Society and the Special Collections Research Center at Bird Library at Syracuse University for releasing photographs for use in this book. An earlier version of chapter 2 appeared in "Italian Women of Industry: The Shoemakers of Endicott, New York, 1914–1935," *Journal of American Ethnic History,* in 1989. Chapter 3 was adapted from "Gender, Domestic Values, and Italian Working Women in Milwaukee: Immigrant Midwives and Businesswomen," in *Women, Gender, and Transnational Lives: Italian Workers of the World,* edited by Donna Gabaccia and Franca Iacovetta (Toronto: University of Toronto Press, 2002).

A number of friends and scholars have taken time to read this manuscript in its various forms over the years. I owe a special debt of thanks to Donna Gabaccia, not only for reading my work many times over, but for years of friendship, encouragement, and inspiration. I am deeply appreciative to Elliott Barkan, who offered advice, editorial comments, and good humor. Suzanne Sinke posed important questions on an early chapter on midwives, and Franca Iacovetta's insights and criticisms were especially helpful in my efforts to understand and articulate the contributions of Milwaukee's midwives and businesswomen. I am especially grateful for the comments and advice made by the anonymous readers at the University of Illinois Press and for the valuable help provided by Christina Walter, acquisitions assistant at the Press. In addition, I would like to thank my sons—Cory Wilson, who helped prepare photographs, and Adrien Wilson, who procured prints and permissions from the Wisconsin State Historical Society—as well as my stepdaughter, Kelsea Erbatu, who commented on an early draft. I am particularly grateful to Anne Barrington, who painstakingly edited every page of this manuscript.

In the course of doing research and writing, I enjoyed the hospitality of friends and relatives. Marty and Terry Huff housed and fed me during research trips to Wisconsin, and Carmelina and Ida Verrico warmed me with hot-water bottles and shots of lemoncello during a cold spring in southern Italy. In South Carolina, the gracious hospitality of Curt and Cleveland Harley allowed me the opportunity to write in solitude overlooking the ocean at Fripp Island.

I would like to thank my colleagues David Spear, Marian Strobel, and former dean A. V. Huff at Furman University for granting me release time to finish this manuscript. Research grants provided by Furman University and the University of Wisconsin Whitewater, a Wisconsin Humanities Grant, and fellowships from the John Ben Snow Foundation, Syracuse University, and the National Italian American Foundation provided financial support for my research. I am especially thankful to the dozens of immigrants and children of immigrants, in Wisconsin and New York, who invited me into their homes and allowed me to interview them.

My deepest thanks go to my family. In all of my educational and professional pursuits, I have had the encouragement of my wonderful parents, Marie and Alex Vecchio. While they were alive, my grandparents, Rose and Joseph Verrico, provided unrelenting support for my work by providing childcare and preparing meals. My children, Adrien and Cory Wilson, and stepchildren, Kelsea Erbatu and Ben Stockwell, have been a constant source of joy and pride. They have patiently understood and supported my efforts to complete this project. My greatest thanks and appreciation go to my husband, John Stockwell, who has lovingly supported me in all my endeavors and was never too busy in his own work as a college president to read drafts, offer advice, and keep up my spirits.

Introduction

IN 1909, Maria and Salvatore Latona and their four children left Bagheria, Sicily, for Milwaukee, Wisconsin. In Milwaukee Salvatore was hired at the Department of Public Works but worked only seasonally. Maria saw an opportunity to contribute to the household earnings by taking in boarders. Hoping to improve their economic status, the couple became small-business owners. Salvatore opened a tavern, and Maria started a grocery store, which she operated from six in the morning until eight at night. The grocery store was located in the couple's basement, making it possible for Maria to earn an income without ever leaving home.[1]

In 1925, fourteen-year-old Bridgetta Bianco dropped out of school in Endicott, New York, to take a job as a shoe worker at Endicott Johnson, the largest employer in central New York. The Bianco family had recently emigrated from the Abruzzi, and, with twelve children, Bridgetta's parents needed her financial assistance. An ambitious and hard-working woman, Bridgetta continued to labor in the factory after her marriage and the birth of her daughter. An activist in the late 1930s, she led her Slavic and Italian co-workers in a walkout at the factory, demanding better wages.[2]

Both women adapted to the economic environment in which they lived, but in different ways. Maria created an opportunity to earn money while remaining at home, adjusting her work life to domestic responsibilities. Bridgetta, on the other hand, worked outside the home, adjusting family responsibilities to the demands of her job. The examples of Maria and Bridgetta reflect a variety of work experiences shared by thousands of Italian immigrant women in the United States at the turn of the century.

These women—merchants, midwives, and laborers—and their stories are the subject of this book. Studies of immigrant laboring women have been the topic of many books and articles, but scholars of Italian immigrant women rarely study Italian merchants and midwives. Moreover, this study focuses on two contrasting locales that have not received much attention from historians: the upper Midwest and rural upstate New York.

The history of women's work and wage earning has contributed greatly to scholars' understanding of immigrant women's lives in America. Conclusions about immigrant women's assimilation and adaptation, independence and autonomy, personhood and identity have been drawn by examining women's work experiences.

Until recently, scholars of Italian American life relied on inherent assumptions about Italian culture and male control of women as a paradigm for understanding Italian women's work and wage-earning experiences in the United States.[3] This paradigm portrays Italian women as submissive wives and daughters who were severely limited by intensely jealous husbands and fathers who carefully guarded and controlled their women, thus restricting them from a variety of employment possibilities. A fuller understanding of southern Italian women has suffered, in large part, by the absence of a careful examination of Italian sources documenting both waged and nonwaged forms of women's work. Thus, Italian women have generally been presented, not as agents, but as passive victims of an intensely patriarchal culture.

Italian sources reveal that in addition to their domestic responsibilities, women in Italy had economic responsibilities to the family that often included work experiences outside the home. A review of the work experiences and gendered divisions of labor in Italy shows that women's participation in waged labor was surprisingly high during the late nineteenth and early twentieth centuries.[4] In fact, the Italian census reveals that more than 30 percent of the Italian labor force from 1871 to 1911 was female.[5]

In both northern and southern Italy, women were involved in the agricultural economy and worked in both waged and nonwaged agricultural labor. Women were employed outside the home in the silk industry in central and northern Italy, for example, while women in villages, small towns, and urban areas operated grocery stores and worked as seamstresses and midwives. Throughout Italy, women's employment was deeply tied to the economic opportunities of the region in which they lived, as it would be in the years following emigration. The regional variation of women's work in Italy as well as the skills they transplanted to America suggests a modest corrective to a scholarship on Italian migrant working women dominated by images of inexperienced and low-skilled laborers.[6]

Moving beyond reductionist theories and conventional portraits of Italian women, this study of immigrant women's work experiences in America explores the factors leading Italian immigrant women to seek certain kinds of occupations while excluding them from others. I explore these complex factors through the prism of immigrant women's work experiences during the early decades of the twentieth century in two regions of the United States: Endicott, New York, and Milwaukee, Wisconsin.

Why Endicott and Milwaukee? I selected these two communities, one on the East Coast and one in the Midwest, because they represent many characteristics found in numerous other American cities. Endicott and Milwaukee offer interesting contrasts in that each city reveals divergent economic and industrial structures that largely represented the range of work experiences among Italian women. In Endicott Italian women earned wages by working outside the home as factory operatives, while in Milwaukee Italian women largely remained at home and earned income by operating businesses and providing services to the ethnic community.

The accounts from Endicott and Milwaukee are representative of immigrant women's work experiences elsewhere in the United States. Endicott, a small city dominated by light industry (shoemaking), utilized female labor, as did other light-industry cities where textile manufacturing was prominent, such as Amoskeag, New Hampshire, and San Antonio, Texas. Significant numbers of immigrant women in the United States were employed in sectors characterized by a growing demand for female workers. In the Northeast, textile manufacturing drew female job seekers from Canada and Europe, while mills in the South recruited native-born women from Tennessee, Georgia, and the Carolinas. San Antonio's garment industry was dominated by Mexican women workers,[7] while Italian and Jewish women made up the majority of female workers in the needle trades in New York, Chicago, Baltimore, and Philadelphia.[8]

Elsewhere, substantial numbers of immigrant women worked in other light industries, such as cigar making and canning. In Ybor City, Florida, Cuban, Spanish, Italian, and African American women worked in the city's booming cigar industry.[9] In southern California, Mexican women worked in fruit and vegetable canneries,[10] as did Italian women in upstate New York.

Dramatically different, Milwaukee had a diverse economy based on commerce, transportation, and industry. Unlike Endicott, Milwaukee's economic opportunities were based primarily on heavy industry, which required a male workforce. Milwaukee is representative of other heavy-industry cities at the turn of the century, such as Buffalo, Birmingham, and Detroit, cities characterized by steel and automotive manufacturing. Milwaukee's heavy industries, however, generated few job opportunities for females. In contrast to New England and the Mid-Atlantic states, Milwaukee had no textile mills, and as a result only a small minority of immigrant women found paid employment outside the home. Nonetheless, as recent scholarship has documented, Italian women did find ways of earning an income while remaining at home—for example, by taking in boarders, doing homework, and starting small businesses.

The range of female work experiences in Endicott and Milwaukee, while reflecting characteristics of the local economy, was affected by other factors contributing to immigrant women's adjustment in an urban/industrial setting. These factors, which I consider independent variables, include the gender segmentation of the workforce, the geographical proximity of workplace to residence, kinship networks, and the impact of the life cycle on women's lives. These factors contributed significantly to immigrant women's inclination to participate in wage labor. In Endicott Italian women entered wage labor at Endicott Johnson, in large part because of favorable conditions in the community and in the factory and as a result of the networking and support systems they created. The division of labor and gender segregation in the workshop, the kinship networks of labor recruitment and childcare, and the geographical settlement patterns of Italians reinforced immigrant women's familial responsibilities and cultural values.

In Endicott immigrant women's work outside the home often raised questions about their roles as wives and mothers. However, conflict seems to have been ameliorated in Endicott because work outside the home did not radically alter traditional gender roles. Furthermore, Endicott Johnson's program of welfare capitalism aided working mothers and reinforced familial values.

Drawn from extensive oral interviews and research data from Endicott and Milwaukee, this study examines the types of work that Italian women engaged in and analyzes immigrant women's work experiences. Women engaged in two types of work: the first developed where a segmented labor market with a growing demand for female workers prevailed. This type of work was closely associated with increasing job opportunities in "female" industries that grew during the second industrial revolution.[11] These female or light industries, which emerged during the nineteenth century and continued to expand into the next century, resulted in work opportunities for women in the textile and garment trades, cigar manufacturing, canning, and shoemaking.

Light industries also hired women for jobs that could be done at home. In New York City, for example, Italian women dominated the field of finishing garments in their tenement homes.[12] Homework materials were handed out at the factory, taken home and worked on, and returned the following day or at the end of the week. The work ranged from the sewing of garments to the making of artificial flowers and feathers to the making of lace and embroidery work.[13]

The second type of work engaged in by Italian immigrant women developed in response to the growing demand and needs of the ethnic enclave. Immigrant women provided services to the evolving ethnic community by taking in boarders, by assisting as midwives, and by operating businesses that served other immigrants. The first of these, providing boarding and lodging, was an economic enterprise that Italian women extended to immigrants from their homeland. For more than half a century, in the late 1800s and early 1900s, the proportion of urban households that at any point in time had boarders or lodgers was between 15 percent and 20 percent.[14] In Homestead, Pennsylvania, for example, a typical Slavic family had from one to four lodgers in their four-room house,[15] and in Providence, Rhode Island, nearly 30 percent of Italian wives between 1915 and 1935 earned additional income by keeping boarders and wage-earning relatives.[16]

Businesswomen and midwives provide other examples of Italian women who responded to the growing demand and needs of the ethnic enclave. While they often differed with respect to educational background and work patterns, businesswomen and midwives shared a common status as immigrant women and as providers of services critical to first-generation Italians in the ethnic neighborhoods. Similar to the family shops operated by Chinese women on the West Coast or the stores and stalls on the East Coast where Jewish women sold food, staples, and household wares,[17] Italian women, too, managed small retail businesses catering to ethnic or American consumers.[18]

Within their ethnic neighborhoods, Italian midwives, like the Mexican midwives in the rural villages of New Mexico and Arizona,[19] went house-to-house delivering the babies of immigrant women who preferred midwife-assisted deliveries by immigrant-speaking midwives rather than by U.S. doctors and hospitals. Businesswomen and midwives both recognized the needs of the immigrant community and achieved economic goals within the boundaries of their ethnic neighborhoods.

Working Out or Earning at Home:
Two Models of Women's Work Patterns

In addressing these female occupational types, I identify two models of women's work patterns. The first is that of women who worked outside the home, such as factory operatives and midwives. They include women such as Bridgetta Bianco, who worked outside the home, adjusting family responsibilities to the demands of her job.

The second model represents Italian women who were motivated to earn income while simultaneously continuing familial and household responsibilities. This model applies particularly to women who owned and operated grocery stores at home, kept boarders, and engaged in homework. Similar to Maria Latona, they created opportunities to earn money while remaining at home, adjusting their work lives to domestic responsibilities.

These occupational types and models of women's work patterns reveal that, as labor migrants in the United States, Italian women invested themselves in patterns of work that were largely the result of economic opportunities. The research data from Endicott and Milwaukee further suggest that while a large number of Italian women's work experiences were shaped by domestic and child-rearing responsibilities, others, such as midwives, often put their work careers above family expectations and familial duties.

Work and wage earning were not new experiences for Italian women in America. Furthermore, not all of the Italian job-seeking women were unskilled, untrained, and uneducated. A large number of Italian women immigrated to the United States with a rich background of work experiences in waged and nonwaged agricultural labor, as silk workers and small-business proprietors, as seamstresses and professionally trained midwives. At the same time, however, Italian women in America were often confronted with new and unfamiliar opportunities for earning money. While many immigrant women became wage earners in large-scale factories, others used their domestic talents to provide lodging and boarding services to their *paesani*. Premigration skills and training combined with postmigration needs and occupational opportunities to shape the lives of Italian women in the United States.

Organization of the Book

In the prologue I review briefly the nature of women's premigration work in Italy. It is widely acknowledged that Italian women were partners in the family economy and were expected to contribute to the economic resources shared by all members.[20] Most often, however, that is understood as non-waged domestic labor. I discuss Italian women's work experiences beyond the domestic household by citing the early works of Louise Tilly and Elda Gentili Zappi as well as more recent studies by Maddalena Tirabassi and Linda Reeder. Drawing from *L'Inchiesta Agraria* and marriage records from the southern village of Santi Cosma e Damiano, I review briefly the work experiences of women, the gendered division of labor, and the regional variations that characterized women's work opportunities in Italy. These accounts confirm that a surprisingly large number of Italian women engaged in waged and nonwaged agricultural labor, business ventures, and labor outside the home in the late nineteenth and early twentieth centuries. The premigration work experiences of Italian women suggest that not all Italian female migrants were unprepared to meet the challenges of a new and dynamic American economy.

Chapter 1 examines immigrant patterns of social networking and chain migration that drew Italians to Endicott, New York, and Milwaukee, Wisconsin. I contrast the economic opportunities available to women in Endicott, a city dominated by light industry, to those in Milwaukee, a city dominated by heavy industry. I also explore another factor that influenced immigrant women's work in the two regions: the institution of an ethnic occupational hierarchy in Milwaukee and the establishment of the Endicott Johnson Corporation in Endicott.

Chapter 2 looks specifically at Italian female wage earners at Endicott Johnson, where immigrant women took factory jobs as shoe workers. The wage-earning opportunities available in Endicott represent a segmented labor market with a growing demand for female workers. In addition to the need for female labor in Endicott, other factors or "independent variables" created favorable conditions attracting immigrant women to factory labor. These include gender segregation in the workshop, kinship networks of labor recruitment and childcare, and the geographical settlement patterns of Italians, all of which accommodated Italian family work traditions. Another important issue is Endicott Johnson's practice of corporate welfare. While welfare capitalism was devised primarily to instill loyalty to the company and curb labor unrest, Endicott Johnson's benevolence created a supportive atmosphere for working mothers, provided them with benefits, and reinforced familial goals and values. I demonstrate that Italian women, both single and married, worked outside the home in wage labor at the Endicott Johnson Corporation—a decision that significantly improved their lives and the lives of their children because of the company benefits provided for working women.

In contrast to the working experiences of immigrant women in Endicott, Italian women in Milwaukee, the subject of chapter 3, largely earned income by engaging in entrepreneurial endeavors, such as keeping boarders and operating restaurants and grocery stores. In Milwaukee, unlike Endicott, opportunities for women to earn outside the home were limited because the city's economic base was primarily heavy industry. The type of work engaged in by Italian women in Milwaukee also developed in response to the growing demands and needs of the ethnic enclave. I stress the role of female entrepreneurs in providing services to the immigrant community while contributing to the community's ethnic identity. Two case studies of Sicilian-born women who owned and operated grocery stores in Milwaukee are presented to illustrate how child-rearing responsibilities and domestic values shaped immigrant lives. The significant size of Milwaukee's Italian community provided Italian women ample opportunities for business endeavors, making it possible for them to combine economic activities with domestic responsibilities.

Immigrant midwives are the subjects of chapter 4. In Milwaukee midwives were similar to businesswomen in that they, too, responded to the growing demand and needs of the ethnic enclave, but were different in that, unlike other working women, they were professional practitioners who did not always fashion their work lives around domestic responsibilities. Italian midwives in Milwaukee were professionally trained and educated women. I explore the training and practice of immigrant midwives, the rituals and traditions associated with midwife-assisted births, and the integral roles played by midwives in the life of the immigrant community. This examination of Italian midwives in Wisconsin suggests that domestic values did not—necessarily or entirely—shape immigrant women's work experiences in the early twentieth century.[21]

The availability of key sources in Endicott and Milwaukee made it possible for me to reconstruct the lives of Italian workingwomen. The Endicott study was greatly enhanced by access to Endicott Johnson employment files,[22] company records, and the George F. Johnson Collection housed at the Special Collections Research Center at Bird Library, Syracuse University. I mined several types of sources for Milwaukee. The Midwives Registration Files in the archives of the Wisconsin State Historical Society and the Milwaukee Public Health Department records provided critical information on midwives, their training and certification. A Wisconsin Humanities Grant shared with Lawrence Baldassaro of the University of Wisconsin, for research on Italians in Milwaukee (1990–91), provided entrée to the Italians of the old

Third Ward, the Italian Community Center, and innumerable hours working with Mario Carini, a local historian of Milwaukee's Italians.

The Wisconsin State census for Milwaukee and the Milwaukee City Directories, along with interviews of immigrants and their children, helped me profile Italian businesswomen and midwives. Research conducted in the southern Italian village of Santi Cosma e Damiano gave me further insight into women's work in rural agriculture. Interviews with women in southern Italy and of immigrants and their children in Endicott and Milwaukee provided incisive and intimate details that can be achieved only through oral history. Oral interviews proved particularly useful for gaining access to the kinds of women's experiences that are never recorded, especially those regarding childbirth.

As an Italian American my ethnic background served me well for gaining entrée into the homes of immigrant Italians and their families. I often started out my interviews by talking about my own family's migration history. These shared experiences positioned me, in some ways, as an insider,[23] particularly when I shared my own difficulties balancing career and family. My interviews ranged from questions about family history in Italy to migration experiences and questions about women's working lives. I asked women in Endicott who worked in the shoe factories very specific questions about why they went to work. We discussed their perceptions of Endicott Johnson management, how corporate paternalism affected their lives, the kind of work they performed, gender segregation in the factories, and what it meant to be a working mother. In Milwaukee I discussed midwifery practices and birth rituals with women who had been assisted by Italian midwives. Second-generation Italians related stories about immigrant mothers who turned front rooms into grocery stores. In both Endicott and Milwaukee, Italian families welcomed me into their homes and shared both joyous events (the birth of a baby, religious festivals) as well as the tragic aspects of their lives (the loss of a child while emigrating, unemployment, and poverty).

Long before I became a student of immigrant women, I was acutely aware of Italian women's work experiences and economic roles in the family. As a young child, I accompanied my Italian-born paternal grandmother, hand-in-hand, along the railroad tracks to Patriarca's, to visit *comare* Maria who operated a bar and restaurant. I remember sitting on a barstool while Maria prepared sandwiches for Italian and Russian railroad workers stopping in for lunch.

On weekends spent with my maternal grandparents in the Italian end of town, I listened attentively to my grandmother's recollections of working in a sewing factory with other Italian women. Armed with her grocery list, I picked up cheese and *cappicola* at Mary's Grocery Store down the street and fresh Italian bread at Carmela Ferro's store around the corner. Writing about Italian grocers in Milwaukee brought back the sights and smells of the little shops operated by immigrant women in their homes on the south end of Cortland. As a teenager, I returned home from school in time to mind the family business, an interior-decorating store that my mother operated across the street from our home, so that she could start dinner for our family of six.

My small-town worldview of Italian women resembles closely what I have uncovered through scholarly research. The determination and experiences of ordinary women like Bridgetta Bianco and Maria Latona, often juggling wage earning with household responsibilities in order to better their lives and the lives of their families, is an experience that is familiar to me and countless other daughters and granddaughters of the immigrant generation.

Prologue:
Before the Crossing

BEFORE IMMIGRATING to the United States, where she worked for several years in a canning company, Emilia Palazzo made and sold cheese from the goats she tended and used the eggs from the chickens she raised as barter for salt, flour, dried fish, and sugar. According to her son, "While my father labored for wages in the United States, my mother tended the land we owned in San Lorenzo and hired local women to harvest the grapes."[1] Gender expectations in Italian society supported women as partners in the family economy and upheld their position of authority in household and domestic decision-making.[2] Emilia Palazzo provides an example of Italian women's nonwaged work in the agricultural economy—a combination of domestic responsibilities and income-producing activities.

From the mid-nineteenth century to the early decades of the twentieth, Italian women were similar to working women in the United States, in that they were overwhelmingly members of the working and peasant classes. Joan Scott and Louise Tilly maintain that while nineteenth-century middle-class women were confined to their proper sphere of domesticity, traditional ideas about women held by peasant and laboring families did not find feminine and economic functions incompatible.[3] In fact, according to the Italian census, more than 30 percent of the Italian labor force from 1871 to 1911 was female, similar to the rates of female employment in the more industrialized countries of northern Europe.[4]

Recent scholarship of Italian peasant women suggests that female wage earning was common in the years coinciding with the great migration of over four million Italians to the United States between the years 1870 to 1914.

The region one lived in determined, to a great extent, the kinds of employment available.

Agriculture employed the largest numbers of women throughout Italy, especially in the northern and central regions of the country. According to the census of 1891 and 1911, the representation of women in agriculture was highest in Piedmont, with 83 women for every 100 men engaged in agriculture. In the northern and central regions of Liguria and the Marche the ratio of female to male agricultural workers was roughly 70, followed by Lazio with 49 and—in the south—Calabria with 45, Puglia with 36, and Sicily with 28.7. According to Maddalena Tirabassi, these figures reflect the use of paid labor in commercial agriculture found in northern Italy.[5] This was especially true in areas where women were recruited to harvest commercial crops such as rice, tobacco, and sugar beets.

An extensive study of the establishment of northern Italy's rice production conducted by Elda Gentili Zappi examines the critical role of women workers in the commercialized production of rice for over five centuries. In 1881, 73,608 persons over the age of fifteen were agricultural wage earners in the rice districts of Vercelli, Novara, and Lomellina. Of these, 37,226 were women.[6] Thousands of Italian women regularly left their towns and villages for seasonal work as agricultural laborers in the rice fields—where they were housed in dormitory-style facilities—and were often the victims of wage exploitation as depicted in the Italian neorealist film *Bitter Rice*.

Women's agricultural work in other areas of Italy, particularly southern Italy and Sicily, is detailed in reports of *L'Inchiesta Agraria* during the 1870s and 1880s. In the area around Naples women worked at sowing the fields and wine harvesting, while in several towns in Reggio-Calabria women harvested olives and citrus and even transported the fruit. The nature of women's work depended on crops indigenous to the region. In the southern Italian village of Santi Cosma e Damiano, located in a mountainous region between Rome and Naples, eighty-two-year-old Maria La Bella discussed her work experiences as a young girl of fifteen during an interview in 2000: "We awoke every morning between 2:00 and 3:00 for the long walk to the fields, where I worked with other young women picking olives in the countryside." In Santi Cosma e Damiano, 26 percent of the married women surveyed in 1936 were classified as *bracciante* (day laborers) who sold their labor on a daily basis, picking grapes and olives.[7]

Women also picked olives and fruit in Chieti and spread manure or carried crops from the fields. In Potenza women were called on to weed and to pick olives and nuts.[8] In the Sicilian village of Nissoria, Rudolph Bell reports that women comprised one-third of all agricultural workers, and in Albareto women were hired by the season as cheese makers and sharecroppers.[9] Typically, a gendered division of labor existed in agriculture. In some areas where fields were far from living areas, women were unable to combine agricultural work with domestic responsibilities. Italian men worked the fields and returned home only once a week. Women, burdened with domestic chores and childcare, stayed behind and did other work such as spinning, weaving, or making handicrafts to supplement the family income.[10] This was true in Ventosa, where women contributed to the family economy by weaving baskets for a regional market.[11] Regional variations in women's participation in agricultural work could be significant, as *L'Inchiesta Agraria* reported, noting that in and around Siracusa (Sicily), women often worked with men in the fields, and in Avola "women were said to be the hardest workers in the region."

In Lombardy, one of the major sources of northern Italian immigration to the United States, a greater diversity of local income-generating opportunities existed in manufacturing. Producing both raw and spun silk thread for the spinning and weaving mills of France, Great Britain, Germany, Switzerland, and North America, women's contribution to the working of silk was clearly defined as wage labor. By the middle of the nineteenth century, silk reeling and throwing gave employment to some 150,000 people in Piedmont and Lombardy.[12] Many workers in northern silk factories were young girls such as Rosa Cavalleri, an Italian migrant from Bugiarno, a silk-making village in Lombardy, who vividly recalls being sent to the *filatoio* (silk factory) at the age of six:

> In the *filatoio* we were winding the silk from one spool to another. Each little girl had about seventeen spools to watch and when the thread to one of those spools broke we had to quick catch the ends and tie a knot. There was one spool above that was so big it took my two arms to reach around it. One woman used to go back and forth behind us to watch and if we didn't tie fast enough she would hit us.[13]

With capitalist development and urbanization taking place in northern and central Italy around 1900, many Italian women had to migrate to cities to earn wages, but even then, they were faced with the impact of industrialization and the economic structure of the urban environment. In her study of the impact of industrialization on women's wage earning, Louise Tilly forges a link between the pattern of women's paid employment and the occupational structure of the city. Between 1881 and 1911, after industrialization began in Milan, Tilly found that the level of female employment declined precipitously. Why the downward curve in women's employment in this newly industrialized city? Industrialization in Milan paralleled the increase in heavy industry and construction, ushering in an era of skilled, specialized, and predominately male labor. "Male" industries included most of the crafts, metal and engineering, construction, transportation, and utilities. The structure of the labor force in Milan had dramatically changed and was marked by a decrease of persons employed in small-scale, poorly capitalized industry as well as a decrease in personal and domestic services—areas that had previously employed large numbers of women. With the advent of industrialization a new economic sector loomed large over the city, one characterized by heavy industry. Ultimately, a clear pattern of gender segregation dominated these industries.[14] Tilly's analysis of Milan's industries importantly reveals that industrialization did not always create employment opportunities for women.

Employment opportunities for women became limited to the cities and to industries characterized as light or "female" employment. In Italy, some women did find employment in specific industries, such as textiles, garment making, tobacco, chemicals, rubber, and paper. In 1861, for example, there were about twenty tobacco factories in northern and central Italy with a predominantly female workforce. In 1880, about 13,707 women were employed in the cigar industry, compared to 1,947 men. The Italian state actually encouraged a tradition in the industry by which mothers could pass on their jobs to their daughters.[15]

Little has been written about the Italian women who owned and operated stores, and their contributions to family and village life are unrecorded. Women engaged in commercial enterprises and provided important services to villages and towns throughout Italy and Sicily. In the nineteenth century the Italian census classified these small-business proprietors or retail merchants under the category "Commerce, Credit, and Services." In 1881, for example, significant percentages of women in the employed population were listed in that category, with Sardinia having the largest percentage of employed women in that sector (55.9), followed by the Marche (51.1) and Piedmont (48.8). Even in the south, percentages of women employed in this sector were high: 46 percent in both Calabria and Sicily.[16] In the Sicilian village of Sutera, Linda Reeder reports that women often ran the family store, while their husbands traveled around the valley buying merchandise. These women were well respected in the village and were generally addressed as *Donna*, a title reserved for the local elite.[17]

At an early age, in addition to household chores, girls learned simple sewing. As they grew older, some girls were taught fine hand sewing and embroidery at schools and convents. Many girls became seamstresses, taking on their own apprentices. The *sarta* (seamstress), a skilled worker, was similar to the midwife and storekeeper, in that she held a distinguished position in the village. Her skill and workmanship were greatly admired, and wealthy women visited her in her home and often hired her to work on a special piece for a dowry.[18] Garment making was important in the provinces around Rome and in Campania, including Naples and surrounding areas.[19] Other seamstresses, such as those who lived away from their families, found employment in urban centers, working in Turin's garment industry in the first half of the twentieth century.[20]

The two professions open to Italian women at the turn of the century were teaching and midwifery. In 1901, women made up about 68 percent of all teachers in Italy (35,344), and by 1922, women comprised 78 percent of all teachers.[21] A profession with a longer history was the practice of midwifery. As late as the mid-1930s, 93 percent of all Italian births still took place at home, with 901 out of 1,000 women aided solely by a midwife.[22] Italian women who were professionally trained midwives attended universities or received practical training in hospitals. Throughout Italy and Sicily, midwives, lay as well as professionally trained, occupied an important position in village life because they performed important functions. Dating back to the Council of Trent in 1546, the Catholic Church granted the midwife official status as having the right to have children baptized. Midwives brought many babies to baptism, provided legal testimony in the case of illegitimate children, and provided expertise in illnesses affecting women and children.[23]

In her study of the Sicilian village of Sutera, Linda Reeder reports that midwives married well and enjoyed the respect of their community. One such woman, who received her diploma in midwifery from the University of Palermo in 1872, married an elementary school teacher and was hired by Sutera's city council and paid over six hundred lire each year to be the village midwife.[24]

Finally, women also engaged in domestic service, work that is often associated with the very poorest of Italian women. According to Maddalena Tirabassi, "to go into domestic service in southern Italy was considered humiliating and a disgrace." Nonetheless, the 1901 census records 19.2 percent of the entire female labor force employed in domestic service, with 9.2 in Calabria, 18.9 in Campania, 23.5 in Basilicata, and 34 in Sicily. According to Tirabassi, most domestics were young unmarried women who had emigrated from the countryside to live with their employers.[25] In small villages, however, local women often worked as domestics for large landowners.[26] According to Carmelina Verrico, "it was customary for the women employed by the local *possidente* to work in their homes during the day and return to their own homes and take care of their families and household responsibilities in the evening."[27]

Evidence gleaned from a brief review of women's work in Italy suggests that work and wage earning were not unfamiliar to Italian women. When Italian women immigrated to the United States, they often came with skills and work experiences that were far more extensive than most scholars of immigrant women have generally acknowledged.[28] In 1919, social investigator Louise Odencrantz first raised the issue of immigrant women's work experiences prior to migration when she reported that about one-half of a group of 176 Italian women living in New York City had contributed to their own support before arriving in America. The Italian women she interviewed had worked outside their homes in rural regions as farmhands or as apprentices to local dressmakers.[29] Similarly, a small, but not insignificant number of immigrant women employed at Endicott Johnson in central New York had also been employed in Italy prior to emigration.[30]

Italian women most often migrated in family groups, but recent scholarship provides evidence that Italian women also emigrated alone.[31] Women took part in labor migrations in order to support themselves, to contribute to the family economy, to save money for a dowry, or to send money back home to help ailing or aged parents. Whether as single women or as mothers and wives, Italian females came to America with more than bundles balanced on their heads—they immigrated with skills and work experiences that they would draw on in their attempts to balance premigration cultural and familial patterns with postmigration economic need and opportunities.

1

Encountering America

IN 1900, sixteen-year-old Catherine D'Aquisto left her family in Porticello, Sicily, for the United States, where she joined an older sister, who offered her a job in her New York bakery. Several years later, another sister called for her, and Catherine left New York for Milwaukee, where she eventually married, raised eight children, and operated a grocery store.[1] In 1908, Amelia Bertoni, who initially immigrated to Scranton, Pennsylvania, was urged by a cousin to relocate to Endicott. Her cousin helped her get a job at Endicott Johnson, where she worked for the next twelve years.[2]

Catherine D'Aquisto and Amelia Bertoni, similar to other immigrants, both male and female, were called to America by relatives who had established themselves earlier. Immigrants relied on personal contacts and communications with friends and relatives, a process of social networking, according to Sam Baily, that often began in the village of origin and continued outward with migration and incorporation into the host society.[3]

Throughout the late nineteenth and early twentieth centuries, women increasingly made up a larger proportion of Italian immigrants. From 1891 to 1900, 22.8 percent of all Italian immigrants were women, a percentage that increased to 39.4 between 1921 and 1930.[4] The majority of Italian female migrants destined for Endicott and Milwaukee immigrated in family groups, but some women immigrated alone to join relatives already in the United States or to rejoin husbands who had immigrated earlier. While most immigrant women's employment represented familial obligation, it would be unwise to conclude that women worked only because economic realities forced them to do so or that women who worked outside the home took no enjoyment in their work experiences.

Undoubtedly, Italian families met harsh economic realities after settling in the United States. Rarely did an individual man or woman earn enough money to provide even a modest standard of living. The Dillingham Commission noted that in 1900, 33.2 percent of first-generation Italian males were laborers, the highest percentage of general laborers for any class of immigrants.[5] These were often seasonal, low-paid street and municipal jobs. Recently arrived immigrants also had prior debts, the cost of passage, and commitments of financial aid to family members remaining in Italy. Even in prosperous periods, writes Alice Kessler-Harris, where one person's income could buy the family's bare necessities, the household relied on the contributions of other members in order to save for a small plot of land or a home.[6]

Italian migrant women, whether single or married with children, employed several strategies to support themselves and their families. These strategies were based, in large part, on the specific environment in which Italians lived. The economic structures of Endicott and Milwaukee at the turn of the twentieth century provided a sharp contrast in opportunities for women's work that ultimately helped shape gender ideologies central to Italian family life.

Economic Opportunities in Endicott and Milwaukee

The economic development of Endicott at the turn of the twentieth century was deeply tied to the evolution of the Triple Cities, composed of Binghamton, Endicott, and Johnson City in Broome County, New York. During the late nineteenth century, two of the largest industries that evolved in Binghamton were the cigar and shoe industries. Both were based upon large-scale production for the national market. However, unlike Milwaukee, a city dominated by heavy industry, Binghamton and the rest of Broome County would be characterized by a variety of light-industrial enterprises. The county's expanding economy attracted European immigrants as well as migrants from rural areas to work in cigar making, in tanneries, and in shoe factories.

Cigar making became the largest industry during the last three decades of the nineteenth century. Nearly one-third of all manufacturing workers were employed in that industry, most of them working in factories that employed more than one hundred people. The cigar industry mostly employed low-paid, unskilled, relatively young migrants from the countryside and, later, foreign immigrants from Ireland and eastern and southern Europe, the majority of whom were females (by 1890, women already comprised 40 percent of the labor force in the cigar industry).[7] However, cigar making declined somewhat at the end of the century, and its leading role in the local economy was replaced by shoemaking.

Mass-production shoemaking signaled an important event in the economic history of Broome County: the establishment of the Endicott Johnson Company, which was to become the largest industry with the greatest number of foreign-born factory operatives in upstate New York. Its history dates to 1854, with the founding of the Lester Brothers Company in Binghamton. In 1888, after continual growth, the company president made plans to expand the shoe business outside the city limits, where the land was parceled and laid out as a village named Lestershire. He also arranged for a well-publicized land auction to attract both shoe workers and investors.[8]

As Lester's business grew, it changed from a family business into a stock company and was reorganized as the Lestershire Boot and Shoe Company. In 1893, the company was reorganized again under the ownership of Henry B. Endicott, a major stockholder.[9] George F. Johnson, a young man who had been the factory's assistant superintendent since 1887, became the new manager of the firm, and in 1900 Johnson became Endicott's partner.

Johnson began to formulate plans for dramatic growth, and in 1901 the company expanded into a nearby rural area located on the north shore of the Susquehanna River, about nine miles west of the city of Binghamton. By mid-1901, the quiet lumbering and farming area developed into an industrial community named Endicott.

In 1902, the Lestershire Boot and Shoe Company was renamed the Endicott Johnson Company and began expanding into the retail sales trade, opening more than a dozen stores throughout upstate New York. Promotional literature emphasized business opportunities and the advantages of locating in Endicott, citing the proximity of the Erie Railroad, with its new passenger and freight depots, and providing pictures of sample houses for working-class and middle-class buyers, described as "comfortable cottages."[10]

Endicott Johnson grew into one of the world's largest shoe companies and the village's largest employer. In fact, between 1900 and World War I, there was constant growth in the company. The construction of the chrome tannery, the upper leather beam house and hide building, the pioneer annex, and the heeling and trimming factories brought hundreds of new workers and their families to Endicott. With massive plant expansion and the influx of thousands of workers, George F. Johnson embarked on a program of corporate welfare in an effort to ameliorate the problems associated with industrial growth. While Johnson's welfare philosophy was similar to that practiced by other Northern corporations and Southern mill owners, Endicott would not become a company town like Ford's or a "mill village" like those found in the textile-producing areas of the Piedmont in North and South Carolina. The Endicott Johnson Corporation, while the largest employer in Endicott, would not be the only employer in Endicott. While it remained a small town dominated by the shoe industry, Endicott would eventually become home to many small businesses and several other firms, including IBM.

The complex industrial life of Milwaukee provides a sharp contrast to the small village of Endicott, a community that was dominated by a single industry at the turn of the century. Nonetheless, Milwaukee and Endicott both experienced at least one important demographic trend in common: they attracted large numbers of European immigrants, among them, Italians.

Italians migrating to Milwaukee at the turn of the century entered an industrial stronghold and a center of commercial capital. Located on one of the largest of the Great Lakes, Milwaukee had two resources that contributed to its development as a major Midwestern port city: the largest bay and the deepest river on the western shore of Lake Michigan.

First settled by Yankee pioneers in the 1830s, the city's population reached six thousand in 1843, four years after the arrival of its first major European immigrants: "Old Lutheran" Germans.[11] Drawn by location and cheap land, German immigrants shaped the city of Milwaukee, making it what one historian calls "the most German City in the most German State in America."[12]

Other Europeans settled in Milwaukee, but no other single group approached Germans in size or influence. By 1850, 64 percent of Milwaukee's population was of foreign birth, and nearly two-thirds of that number had been born in Germany.[13] Irish immigrants comprised 15 percent of the city's population, and in addition Norwegians, Danes, Swedes, and Bohemians were calling Milwaukee home by mid-century.

During the early 1850s, Wisconsin emerged as an important center of wheat production. Milwaukee shipped the grain that was grown on the agricultural frontier, making up nearly three-fourths of the tonnage carried by Wisconsin's railroads in the early 1860s.[14] In the years preceding the Civil War, Milwaukee's leading industries included flour-milling, meatpacking, tanning, and brewing. Two of these important industries, meatpacking and tanning, were based on the large numbers of cattle and hogs raised by Wisconsin farmers. In 1847, German immigrant Guido Pfister opened the Buffalo Leather Company and was later joined by his friend and fellow countryman, Fred

Vogel. By the 1870s, the majority of leather works in Milwaukee were owned by Germans, contributing to its position as the largest tanning center in the world.[15]

While German immigrants were leading figures in the tanning trade, they were practically the only figures in Milwaukee's most renowned industry: brewing. In 1856, there were twenty-six breweries in Milwaukee manufacturing 75,000 barrels of ale and beer. The Best Brewing Company (later Pabst) was established in 1844, after the family transplanted the brewing business they had operated in Mettenheim, Germany. August Krug's brewery, founded in 1849, was eventually taken over by an employee, Joseph Schlitz, who brewed "the beer that made Milwaukee famous." Valentin Blatz, a Bavarian brewer's son, created the Plank Road Brewery, which was bought out in 1855 by another German brewer, Frederick Miller, who ultimately made the Miller Beer Company the largest brewery in Milwaukee.[16] By the late 1860s, the brewing industry had expanded to serve a national market, and beer brewing emerged as one of the most important industries in the city. In 1890, the federal census ranked beer first (by value) on the list of local products.[17]

During the mid- to late-nineteenth century, Milwaukee witnessed a dynamic transition from commercial to industrial capitalism. Similar to other Great Lakes cities, Milwaukee became an important industrial center for producing iron and steel. A growing national rail network, cheap land, the presence of iron ore deposits in nearby Dodge County, and the presence of local entrepreneurs with investment capital made Milwaukee a prime location for iron and steel mills. By mid-century, the city emerged as an iron capital, with industries like the Bay View Iron Mill specializing in iron rails and providing employment for nearly two thousand men. Growing even faster was metal fabrication. The value of durable goods turned out by the city's machine shops, foundries, and forges soared from $5,568,445 in the 1890 census to $14,495,362 in 1900, replacing beer as the leading local industry. The Edward P. Allis Company, a leading manufacturer of flour-mill equipment, sawmill machinery, and steam engines operated a massive plant in West Allis, a suburb south of the city created for the massive plant. In 1901, the company combined with two Chicago firms and one Pennsylvania concern to form the Allis-Chalmers Company.[18]

Increasingly, the city's industrial growth depended on a stable and steadily growing workforce. Wage earners rose from 8,433 in 1869 to 20,886 in 1879 and to 38,850 in 1889, an increase of 360 percent in just twenty years. By 1880, industrial workers made up 44.6 percent of the local labor force, the sixth highest concentration in urban America. Milwaukee's industrial workforce was comprised overwhelmingly of immigrant laborers. Ninety-three percent of the workforce of the Bay View Iron Mill, for example, was made up of European migrants.[19]

The state of Wisconsin, as well as local industrialists, played an important role in attracting Europeans to Milwaukee. In the 1870s and 1880s a state agency, though largely interested in agricultural settlement, advertised in northwestern Europe for factory workers. Thousands of pamphlets were sent abroad in the hope of attracting immigrants from England, Belgium, Holland, France, the Scandinavian countries, and Germany. Pamphlets advertised work opportunities at the rolling mills, breweries, tanning factories, machine shops, and the factories of the woodworking, clothing, cigar, and shoe industries, all of which needed skilled workers.[20] Industrialists, like Eber B. Ward of the Milwaukee Iron Company, for example, imported skilled workers from Staffordshire, England, a center for iron and steel manufacturing, for building and operating his Milwaukee plants. The largely British workforce was joined by Scottish and Welsh workers, who also emigrated from the United Kingdom to work in the Bay View Iron Mills.[21] In 1881, Milwaukee cigar manufacturers sent special agents to Bohemia to recruit craftsmen for breaking a strike of skilled cigar makers. In 1884, the Window Glass Company of Bay View recruited glassblowers from Belgium, Germany, France, and England.[22]

Many of the unskilled workers who immigrated to Milwaukee in the late nineteenth century were recruited by agents in New York and Chicago, who placed them in lumber camps, mines, railroad construction, and factories. In the 1880s, when Italians founded a small colony in Milwaukee near the yards of the Chicago and North Western Railroad, the Wisconsin Bureau of Labor and Industrial Statistics reported that a "New York Labor and Construction Company had brought many of them from Europe to work on Wisconsin's railroads."[23]

While Germans continued their demographic dominance in Milwaukee, Poles, attracted largely by jobs in unskilled labor, settled beside them. By 1910, Poles made up 22 percent of the city's foreign-born population, making Milwaukee one of the largest centers of Polish settlement in America, along with Chicago, Detroit, Cleveland, and Buffalo.

In the late nineteenth and early twentieth centuries, the trend in Milwaukee shifted away from northern and western European immigrants and toward southern and eastern European immigrants. Slovaks, who settled in Milwaukee around 1880, were among the most numerous. Similarly, in Endicott southern and eastern European immigrants made up the largest ethnic groups in the late nineteenth and early twentieth centuries.

In the early 1880s, Russian Jews, escaping both poverty and pogroms, arrived in Milwaukee. They were preceded by a large number of German Jews who were quite successful. German Jews in Milwaukee had established themselves as merchants and manufacturers of dry goods and garments. They were investors in the Great Lakes mines and local real estate. By 1900, practically all thirteen clothing factories and shops in Milwaukee were Jewish owned, and three of the largest dry goods firms, including Gimbels', were owned by German Jews.[24]

After 1870, however, Jewish immigration came from eastern Europe rather than Germany and made up the ranks of the industrial poor. These were largely *shtetl* Jews who engaged in petty retailing as grocers and itinerant traders. East European Jews, unlike the German Jews, had little formal education, and a large number of them were unskilled. At first, their German brethren responded generously, helping the newcomers find jobs and housing. Adolf Rich, a German Jewish shoe manufacturer, headed a society to help East European Jewish immigrants find employment. The Milwaukee Jewish Industrial Aid Society found jobs for 340 Romanian Jews and, by 1904, had arranged employment for another 600 carpenters, tanners, tinsmiths, machinists, and laborers.[25]

Other "new" immigrant groups—Italians, Greeks, Serbs, Slovenes, and Croats—migrated to the city in search of work in Milwaukee's booming industrial economy. In 1890, immigrants and their children already made up 86.4 percent of the community's population, earning Milwaukee a designation as one of the most foreign cities in America. Foreign immigration contributed to the boom in the city's population, which numbered 373,000 in 1910, making it the twelfth largest city and the fifteenth largest metropolitan area in the country.[26]

Strikingly different demographic and industrial patterns evolved in Endicott. The increase in population was a result of the growth of the Endicott Johnson Company and the employment opportunities available at the shoe factory. Endicott grew from a small, sleepy village of 2,408 in 1910 to nearly 10,000 by 1920—the majority of whom were factory workers.

Beginning in the late 1890s, the company employed increasing numbers of immigrants from southern and eastern Europe. By the early 1920s, company records show that foreign-born workers made up 33 percent of the total workforce (4,519 foreign-born out of a total workforce of 13,665). Slavs comprised the largest immigrant ethnic group, making up around 20 percent of the labor force in 1922. In addition to the foreign-born, a large and ever-growing number of native-born children of immigrant parentage were also employed for the company. By the mid-1930s, half of the firm's workers were immigrants or the children of immigrants.[27]

Among these were Italians, some of whom originally settled in Binghamton, later moving to Endicott following the expansion of the shoe business. Italians, who comprised a little over 1,000 of the foreign-born population in Endicott (41 percent of 2,491), made up a growing number of the immigrant workforce at Endicott Johnson.[28]

Italian immigration to Endicott followed two patterns: one a direct route from Italy characterized by patterns of social networking and the other comprised of secondary migrations from other regions in the United States. Parish records from St. Anthony of Padua, the Italian Catholic Church in Endicott, indicate that the greatest number of Italians emigrated from Alberobello, in the province of Bari. Patterns of chain migration are evident in towns and villages in and around Bari, from Campobasso, and from several small villages in the province of Caserta, Reggio Calabria, and western Sicily.[29]

One of the most striking features of Italian migration has been the predominance of large village chains or social networks.[30] As John Briggs puts it, "The brother calls the brother, the friend calls the friend, and thus it is the way they all go."[31] Similar patterns evolved throughout the Triple Cities as Italian migrants made their way to central New York for jobs at Endicott Johnson. They found jobs at the shoe factories and wrote home to friends and relatives in Italy. Typically, a worker obtained a job through a family member or a close friend. Mothers, fathers, cousins, aunts, and uncles used kinship networks to help family members get jobs. As one Italian summed it up, "That's how they did it in those days; they helped each other out. If you had a cousin working, you'd get a job."[32]

In 1911, Frank Allio left Palermo, Sicily, to live with an uncle in Rochester. Three months later he was called by *paesani,* who encouraged him to come to Endicott for work at the shoe factory. In no time at all, Allio obtained a job at Endicott Johnson. In an interview he explained that "at that time you didn't have to go to the office for a job. You could go inside of the factory and ask a boss there on the floor for a job, and if he needed somebody, he'd hire you."[33] Frank met and eventually married another Endicott Johnson worker, a young Sicilian immigrant who worked in the stitching department.

Mary Vallone Monticello, who followed her Italian parents' path into the factory, recalled that "my mother and father immigrated first to Rochester and then to the coal mining regions of Pennsylvania. A friend encouraged my father to come to Endicott, where safe jobs with steady employment were available." Monticello and his family of ten relocated in Endicott, where he and his wife and several of their children spent their working lives in the shoe factories.[34]

Beginning in the early years of the twentieth century, Italians took jobs at Endicott Johnson and settled permanently in the neighborhoods surrounding the factories. Newly arrived Europeans settled on the north side of Endicott, where Italians lived in neighborhoods adjacent to those inhabited by Slavs and Slovaks. Concentrated in a seven-block area called "the nob," ethnic neighborhoods peered down over the site of a vast array of factories and tanneries.

Italians migrating to the Triple Cities in central New York during the late nineteenth century were first drawn to employment possibilities in a variety of light industries in Binghamton. As the century progressed, increasing numbers of Italians found employment at Endicott Johnson. As the company expanded its operations outside the city of Binghamton into the undeveloped lands to the west, Johnson City and Endicott were established. Ultimately, Endicott became the center of the shoe industry. As a result, Italian migration to Endicott was the result of specific labor needs at the Endicott Johnson factories. At the same time, Italians were immigrating to Milwaukee, not because of any singular industry but because of the diversity of opportunities that accompany a growing urban area—from industry to construction to service and business endeavors.

Italians in Milwaukee and Endicott

Milwaukee's Italian community numbered only about four hundred at the end of the nineteenth century but grew rapidly as large numbers of Sicilians settled there after 1900. Fishing villages, such as Sant'Elia, near Palermo, sent hundreds of their native children to Milwaukee. In 1889, the Balistreri family prompted a migration chain of villagers from Sant'Elia when Gaetano Balistreri, his cousin Joseph Alioto, and Vincenzo Catalano emigrated. Catalano's brother had settled in Milwaukee several years earlier and called for them. They were followed shortly thereafter by many other members of the large Balistreri family, as well as the Busalacchis, Machis, and other Sant'Elians.

The mass immigration of southern Italians to the United States at the turn of the century contributed to a substantial growth in Milwaukee's foreign-born population. In a burgeoning city of nearly 374,000, Italians numbered 5,000 of Milwaukee's foreign-born in 1910.[35] After 1900, Sicilians made up 65 percent of the city's Italian population. Twenty percent came from southern Italy, while 15 percent came from central and northern regions of the country.[36] Northern Italians joined a small group of compatriots who had begun arriving in Milwaukee in the 1850s and consisted largely of males from Tuscany and Liguria. These early migrants were primarily artisans, who, during the 1860s and 1870s, distinguished themselves in the city by their work in marble and mosaics, as terrazzo artisans and wood and stone carvers. In the 1890s, Italian artisans decorated the Milwaukee Public Library and other landmark buildings in the city with marble and tile imported from Italy. Many of these early Italian settlers were artisans involved in the manufacture of statuary and owned and operated three of the four statuary companies in the city.[37]

Similar to patterns in Endicott, many Milwaukee Italians had immigrated to other American destinations before settling permanently in Milwaukee. For example, Josephine Rampolla, daughter of immigrant Anna Torretta, explains that "my mother first immigrated to Mississippi from Sicily in the 1890s, where she was employed as an agricultural worker picking beans before a second move brought her to Milwaukee."[38] Vito DiCristo came to America in 1907 from the region of Bari, called by a *paesano* to labor in the coalfields of West Virginia. "After working there for three years and surviving near-death explosions," he stated, "I took up another friend's invitation to join him in Milwaukee, where I could get a safer job on the railroad."[39]

Beginning in the 1890s, Italians settled in the city's Third Ward, the area lying between the Milwaukee River and Lake Michigan, south of downtown. Known as the "Bloody Third," the ward was first inhabited by the Irish, who moved out to the west side during the 1870s and 1880s. A catastrophic fire in 1892 destroyed twenty square blocks of the ward and left nearly two thousand people homeless. The Irish abandoned the ward, while Italians succeeded them, establishing a community in the burned-out district.[40]

Three distinct groups settled there: The most numerous were Sicilians from the province of Palermo, which included Porticello, Santa Flavia, Sant'Elia, Aspra, and Bagheria. A second group came from the province of Messina, especially from the towns and villages along the coast from Tusa to Milazzo: Santo Stefano di Camastra, Sant'Agata di Militello, Naso, and Capo d'Orlando. A third group emigrated from the province of Trapani and from the little island of Marettimo. Several more emigrated from the provinces of Girgenti and Siracusa. The Italians from the provinces of southern and central Italy came chiefly from the Puglie (Bari and Foggia), Abruzzi (Chieti and Aquila), and Campania (Naples, Salerno, and Avelline). A group of Tuscans came almost entirely from the area between Florence and Pisa.

As Italians settled in the Third Ward, village clustering took place: Sicilians from Bagheria settled on Jackson Street, and those from Santo Stefano di Camastra on Milwaukee Street. Immigrants from Porticello lived next to each other on Cass Street, and many of those from Bari settled on Jefferson Street.[41]

Northern Italians continued to live apart from the Sicilians in the Third Ward and instead settled in the Bay View area and among the Germans on the near south side of town. Bay View, located just south of the city, was home to a small colony of northern and central Italians who lived within walking distance of their work in the iron mills.[42] Their immigration began at about the turn of the century and peaked in the 1910s and early 1920s. By 1920, about one thousand Italians lived in Bay View in a small ethnic enclave near British-born and Irish workers. The largest Italian settlement in Milwaukee, however, continued to be the Third Ward, where Sicilians took advantage of the commercial and industrial opportunities between the river and the lake.

In both Endicott and Milwaukee, Italians settled in areas closest to their work, creating ethnic enclaves of Italians from similar regions and towns.

Immigrants, Gender, and Occupational Opportunities in Milwaukee and Endicott

Census data indicate that the largest number of initial Italian settlers in Milwaukee and Endicott were males. While some Italian women immigrated alone, the majority came as members of family groups or to reunite with husbands who had established themselves earlier. The earliest Italian male immigrants, whether single or married with wives left behind, rented sleeping rooms from their compatriots or lived in boarding houses. They worked with pick and shovel in the streets or on the railroad. A great number of Italian males in Milwaukee worked for the sanitation department or on the coal docks. Others found steadier employment in tanneries, the electric car lines, and the Gas Light Company. Italian males began moving into better-paying jobs in the second decade of the twentieth century, finding work in the foundries or steel works such as the Allis-Chalmers Company, Falk Manufacturing, and the Rolling Mills of Bay View.

The first wave of Italian males was largely unskilled workers who earned the lowest wages in Milwaukee. According to official Milwaukee City Service Commissioners' reports for the years 1896 to 1913, there were 114 Italians on the employment rolls, and only 11 were listed as skilled workers, compared with 103 unskilled laborers.[43] The average Italian male's wage was between a dollar and a half and two dollars a day, though laborers rarely worked a full year. Indeed, few laborers worked in the winter months, when outdoor work on streets and railroads stopped almost entirely, and Italians (and other recent arrivals) were among the first let go. The typical Italian male worked nine months a year and earned an annual salary of about three hundred to four hundred dollars. The average earnings of native-born males in Milwaukee was $539; those of immigrant men $416. Italian males earned the lowest wages.[44]

In addition to low-paying seasonal work, the City Service Commissioners' reports documented another serious problem that limited the number of higher-paying city jobs available to Italian immigrants: illiteracy. Of 323 Italians who applied for a city job between 1896 and 1913, 136 were literate in Italian only; 61 were literate in both Italian and English; and 126 could neither read nor write in either language.

In both cities, Italian males faced serious obstacles in securing a job and advancing in a job. As one of the last immigrant groups to enter Milwaukee's diverse population, Italians were confronted with a labor market that was dominated by ethnic patronage. Germans owned and operated a large number of businesses and industries in Milwaukee and, as a rule, hired other Germans. German, English, Irish, and Polish immigrants—all of whom had become factory foremen—brought their own compatriots into the shops, and immigrant aid societies functioned as clearing houses for jobs.[45] As in the example of Germans Jews who helped secure jobs for Jews from eastern Europe, individuals often functioned as informal employment agents for their own ethnic group.

In a study of Milwaukee's industries, historian Gerd Korman relates how the ethnic hierarchy functioned in Milwaukee's hiring practices. Korman maintains that the city's English- and foreign-language newspapers informed workers about employment opportunities, and agents of companies recruited workers of selected ethnic groups when their plants needed more men. In German and Polish neighborhoods, for example, the saloonkeepers often charged fees for finding employment for beer-drinking customers.[46]

Italians were relegated to the bottom of the ethnic occupational hierarchy, but they were not the only late-coming group so affected. In a study of African American migration to Milwaukee between 1870 and 1914, historian

Joe William Trotter found that migrating Southern blacks were relegated to the lowest positions in the city, filling jobs in domestic service and as common laborers. Racist attitudes and practices of both industrialists and labor unions blocked African American entrance into industrial jobs, making employment even more difficult for blacks than for Italians.[47]

Italians in Endicott also faced an ethnic occupational hierarchy in the shoe industry. According to census data, by 1925, 76 percent of all Italian-born males residing in Endicott worked at Endicott Johnson, where most began their working careers in the lower positions.

Compared with native-born workers, Italian males who worked for the company occupied low positions in the factory hierarchy and received equally low wages. Men's work in the factories ranged from tanning, which was considered the least desirable, to cutting, regarded as the most desirable job by factory workers. Cutting required coordination and precision, while tanning required physical strength and the stamina to tolerate rotting hides and harsh chemicals.[48]

Slavs and Italians were generally overrepresented in low-paid tannery jobs, while the best factory jobs—upper leather cutting, Goodyear stitching, bed lasting, and edge trimming—generally went to native-born workers. Though Italians faced an ethnic occupational hierarchy within the factory, they did not confront hiring practices that kept them out of the shoe factories all together. Hiring practices may have favored native-born workers for the better jobs, but no one, regardless of ethnic background, was turned away from employment at Endicott Johnson.

While large numbers of Italian men were unskilled laborers in both Milwaukee and Endicott, there were significant numbers of men who were engaged in petty retailing and a larger number of tradesmen and artisans. In addition, records from the Milwaukee City Directories between 1900 and 1910 reveal several artists, musicians, and sculptors, as well as schoolteachers, pharmacists, a physician, a bank president, an optician, a truant officer, and an Italian Consul. While few in number, these professionals represented successful men who would eventually emerge as *prominenti* in the ethnic community.

One business endeavor became especially important not only for its economic impact within the Italian community but also for its prominence in the city as a whole. Opportunities in wholesaling emerged as the growing colony created a demand for specialized products, and Sicilians became leaders in the produce business. Often beginning as fruit peddlers, they settled near the city's produce distributors on Commission Row, conveniently located in the Third Ward. Eventually, they amassed enough capital to create their own wholesale distributorships. The Battista and Catalano brothers were two of the first families who had established themselves in this way at the turn of the century. They were later joined by other Sicilians—Pastorino and Schiappacasse, Maglio, Cianciolo, Gagliano, Battaglia, D'Amore, Patti, Busalacchi, and Jennaro—who also became successful in the wholesale fruit and produce business. By 1910, Sicilian-born immigrants had replaced the German monopoly of wholesale distributors on Commission Row.

Italians also dominated the business landscape on the north side of Endicott, where they established restaurants, bakeries, and grocery stores and provided services as barbers, tailors, and butchers. However, the number of Italian businesses in Endicott was dramatically lower than the number of Italian-owned businesses in Milwaukee, a result of several factors. The Italian community of Endicott was decidedly smaller than that of Milwaukee (less than one-fifth the size); thus, it could not support the number of business endeavors that eventually emerged in Milwaukee. In addition, the dominance of the Endicott Johnson Corporation attracted Italians to that area for one particular kind of employment—factory work. For Italians with ambition and business acumen, the attraction of a city like Milwaukee—urban and ethnically diverse—offered greater entrepreneurial opportunities.

In both cities, however, Italians were the most numerous of the late-arriving immigrant groups, and thus, while the occupational structure of the two cities provided jobs for Italians, traditions of ethnic patronage relegated them to the lowest rung on the ladder of economic mobility.

Making It in America: Italian Women in Endicott and Milwaukee

As immigrants to the cities and newcomers to American life, Italian women often faced occupational and ethnic discrimination, as did their male counterparts, but unlike males, women were further limited by a high degree of gender segregation in the labor market, which characterized industrial employment at that time.

In 1900, over a million women in the United States worked in factories at jobs considered appropriate for female workers. About half of the labor force in the textile mills and tobacco factories and a substantial minority in shoe-making, food processing, and other light industries were women. These included foreign-born women and their daughters, who constituted over half of the American workforce of female wage earners before 1900 and slightly less than half of all female wage earners in 1920.[49] The same cities that generated factory work for women, particularly the textile and garment industry, also offered women work that could be finished at home, thus providing thousands of immigrant women with homework for large-scale manufacturers.

For most immigrant women, however, their work experiences in the United States depended heavily upon what they found here. At the turn of the century, Milwaukee and Endicott became destinations for thousands of Italian immigrants. There, they would confront dynamic cities experiencing rapid economic growth and industrial transformation, complicated by a labor market dominated by ethnic patronage.

Italians settling in these cities responded in various ways to their new environment. The economic structures of Endicott and Milwaukee at the turn of the twentieth century provided different employment opportunities for both men and women. Regardless of contrasting economic structures and employment opportunities, Italians learned to mediate their Old World culture with New World realities. In Endicott and Milwaukee alike, Italians were relegated to the bottom of the ethnic occupational hierarchy. However, in both regions, Italian immigrants would find support and strength in their ethnic neighborhoods and in their cultural traditions. They were neither the uprooted, dislocated peasants portrayed in Oscar Handlin's 1951 study nor the traditionalists suggested in Rudolph Vecoli's examination of Italian *contadini* in Chicago.[50] Some attempted to transplant and preserve Old World traditions, while others consciously rebelled against Old World values. The level of success that immigrants achieved in their new environment was not totally molded by their premigration past or limited by the American environment; it was, rather, a combination of cultural traditions and changing values.

In the following chapters I discuss the economic opportunities that immigrant women encountered in Endicott and Milwaukee. Each city was different, and so too were Italian women's work experiences. Regardless of how they earned income, however, Italian women in both cities faced the challenge of negotiating their working lives with their responsibilities as daughters, wives, and mothers.

2

Gender, Economic Opportunities, and Italian Women Workers in Endicott

Most of the women here worked. I came from Pennsylvania and there was no place to work there or maybe mothers would be working there too. Here [Endicott] it was a regular parade of women going to work. . . . You could hear those heels clicking on the sidewalk . . . all the women going to work in the morning.
—Rose Marca, 1982 interview with Nancy Grey Osterud
  (Binghamton, N.Y., Broome County Immigration Project)

HELEN DECECO VENTURINO, the daughter of a schoolteacher and an Associate Judge of the Supreme Court in Pergola, Italy, lost her father at the age of three. Helen attended school in Rome, where she learned fancy stitching, but later immigrated to the United States with her mother and siblings to live with her uncle in Endicott, New York. At the age of fifteen, Helen married and a year later gave birth to a son. When the baby was two months old, her husband deserted her and refused to support Helen unless he could have the child. In 1918, with the help of her uncle, Helen was hired in the fine welt edge trimming department at Endicott Johnson. Helen's husband signed an agreement not to take their son as long as she did not require him to support them.[1]

Italian women arriving in Endicott in the early years of the twentieth century found a small community dominated by one major industry, the Endicott Johnson Corporation. By 1925, Italian-born women and their daughters working in the Endicott Johnson factories comprised 96 percent of the Italian female wage laborers in Endicott.[2]

In this chapter I examine Italian women who became wage earners in the shoe factories during the early decades of the twentieth century. These were immigrant women and the daughters of immigrants who embraced new employment opportunities within a largely Italian social and cultural milieu. They represent the first model of women's work patterns outlined in the introduction: women who worked outside the home.

At the turn of the century, immigrant women sought employment for many reasons. Young Italian girls worked to support themselves or to contribute to the family's income. Italian wives went out to work to help supplement a husband's low wages or seasonal unemployment; single women, widows, or women who had been deserted by their husbands, like Helen Venturino, sought employment to support themselves and their children.

Immigrant women and their daughters worked in Endicott, in large part because the need for additional income was created by the low wages of husbands and fathers. Even though Endicott Johnson wages were relatively high in comparison with other shoe firms in the nation,[3] immigrant workers' wages were lower than native-born workers because of the low positions they occupied in the factory hierarchy. Eventually, Italians made their way into the more skilled and higher-paying factory and tannery jobs, but it took several decades before that happened.

In Endicott working-class family ties and patterns of assistance among Italians were reciprocal arrangements between children and parents. Children often worked to help support the family but parents often invited their newly married children to live with them until they had saved enough money to purchase their own home. This arrangement often lasted for several years. In the Locco residence, for example, fifty-four-year-old Anthony and his wife, Rose, provided a home for their three school-aged children, as well as a married daughter, their son-in-law, and grandchild. Rose looked after her grandchild so that her daughter could work at Endicott Johnson. The Mangini family, with six children of their own, also had a married daughter, son-in-law, and grandchild living with them. Maria Mangini, similar to Rose Locco, took care of her daughter's infant son while she, too, worked at the shoe factory. Patterns of reciprocity utilized in Italian households worked for the economic benefit of both parents and children.

For the first wave of Italian immigrants who settled in Endicott and took jobs in the shoe factories, wages were low, and the pressure for additional family members to work was great. Further burdened by the heavy cost of immigrating to America and setting up households, Italian families depended on the labor of either the mother or working-age children, often both.

Italian women perceived their contributions to the family's wages as a requirement because they believed that they were unable to make ends meet on one pay envelope.[4]

Several factors attracted Italian women to factory labor in Endicott: the economic structure of the local economy, the gender segmentation of the shoe industry, the proximity between home and work, kinship patterns of labor recruitment and childcare, and Endicott Johnson's policies toward working mothers.

Economic Structure of the Local Economy

While the exact number of Italian women workers at Endicott Johnson is unknown, employment cards exist for 475 Italian female employees (foreign-born and second-generation) between 1914 and 1935. Information provided by the company's employment records—along with census data, company records, and interviews with Endicott Johnson employees—helped me to re-create important aspects of immigrant women's lives and work experiences. What evolves from this data is a complex history of women's migration and work experiences in Endicott. Employment records reveal that, while some Italians immigrated directly to Endicott, many attempted to make it in America in previous locations. For others, Endicott was one more stop on their way to yet another American destination.[5]

Employment records provide an excellent source for determining nativity, age, marital status, previous work experiences, and employment history of Endicott Johnson employees. Company records and the *E-J Workers Review*, a monthly publication printed for company employees, chronicle the participation of working women in company-sponsored organizations and social events, thus contributing to a fuller understanding of the meaning of work for immigrant women.

The brief information provided on Endicott Johnson employment cards raises many unanswered questions about women workers. Angelina Franciscone, for example, worked only four months at Endicott Johnson before "leaving town" in 1921 at the age of eighteen.[6] Previously, she had been employed in Italy; had she been an agricultural worker or a domestic servant? Could she have worked in the silk mills in northern Italy, or might she have been a seamstress in a southern village? The employment card notes that she was single, so she may have been traveling with her family to another destination or joining a friend in some other town. Perhaps she was betrothed to an Italian man living elsewhere in the United States. And what brought twenty-two-year-old Nicolette Fiore to Endicott? She had been employed at a tailor shop for two years before working in the shoe factories, which suggests that she probably lived somewhere else in the United States before a second or even a third move brought her to Endicott. Unfortunately, she was discharged after two years of working in the heeling department for being an "unsteady worker."[7] Why did Grace Colonna suddenly "stop showing up for work"? Perhaps, like many other married women with children, she could no longer balance responsibilities for her three children, who remained at home while she worked in the factory.[8]

According to available records, Italian women workers represented females at various stages of the life cycle: girls as young as fourteen who disliked school and dropped out or those helping to support their families worked in the factory.[9] Single women and widows often labored to support themselves, but nearly all women, especially young wives and mothers with children, worked to contribute to the family economy. Italian women were commonly transient workers, moving from one department to another, taking frequent leaves (and subsequently being "reinstated") as a result of pregnancy and child-rearing responsibilities.

A profile of Italian women wage earners in Endicott presents some important challenges to the traditional interpretations of Italian immigrant women in America. Perhaps the most important issue this study raises is the pattern of married Italian women working outside the home in factory labor. In reconstructing a statistical overview of immigrant women's employment at Endicott Johnson, it is clear that patterns of Italian married women's labor-force participation are consistent with general patterns of married women's labor-force participation in other cities dominated by light industry.

Between 1914 and 1935, the employment cards of 475 Italian women reveal that 57.7 percent were married (including 7.5 percent of women who entered the factories as single but married while employed there). Widows accounted for 1.4 percent of all workers, and the remaining 40.9 percent were listed as single. Records show that when Italian women workers are compared to Slavic women workers, for example, Italians had greater numbers of married working women in the workforce than did Slavs (42.6 percent of the Slavic women were married).

Adeline Alimonti's employment record was typical of that of many Italian working mothers. After immigrating to the United States in 1914, she took a job at Endicott Johnson, where she continued working after her marriage. As she began having children, her work at the factory became more infrequent and sporadic. Finally, after years of intermittent employment, she dropped out of the workforce following the birth of her ninth child.[10]

Exactly what percentage of married Italian women worked outside the home is unclear. Analysis of Endicott census data in 1925, for example, shows that 22 percent of Italian-born married women worked outside the home (81 of 374). But the accuracy of these numbers is questionable, since a large number of women with employment cards never appear in the census at all, and when they do, many of them are listed as having no occupation.

In the following sections, I outline the factors contributing to women's participation in wage labor. While these conditions existed in Endicott, New York, many of these factors are representative of circumstances at a number of light industries existing elsewhere in the United States in the early decades of the twentieth century.

Gender Segmentation of the Shoe Industry

> We have nine children in the family. My father works in the tannery; he cannot afford to feed us. So I have to get a job.
> —quoted in Ross McGuire and Nancy Grey Osterud, *Working Lives*

In December 1919, 3,962 female employees accounted for approximately 28 percent of Endicott Johnson's 14,198 workers. As the overall workforce grew to roughly 15,000 by 1927, women made up 35 percent of the labor force. Endicott Johnson was an enterprise that employed women to fill jobs that had been long considered "women's work."

Beginning in the late 1910s and early 1920s an increasing gender division of labor provided jobs specifically designated as women's work. In part, this can be traced to the history of the New England shoe industry itself. In the late eighteenth century the recruitment of female labor in the shoe industry was seen as "a natural evolution of women's abilities as needleworkers." According to historian Mary Blewett, women were recruited to perform only a small part of the work, the sewing of the upper part of the shoe. The introduction of a division of labor represented a major change in the mode of shoe production, and the work assigned to women took on social meanings appropriate to their gender.[11]

The gender division of labor continued in shoemaking as the shoe industry made the transition from small craft-centered shops to the factory. Alice

Kessler-Harris writes that, as the shoe industry as a whole mechanized, the proportion of women among shoe operators crept higher and higher. In 1870, women had been only 5 percent of the labor force in the shoe industry, but by 1910 they were nearly 25 percent.[12] The shoe industry provided a gender segmentation of labor that included tasks identified and accepted as women's work. One of the most important factors contributing to a substantial female workforce at Endicott Johnson was the nature of the shoe industry itself, a light industry generating gender-specific employment opportunities for women. Immigrant women were stitchers, operating sewing machines controlled by a foot treadle and stitching seams on canvas or leather uppers or on linings. They also worked in the cutting rooms, lacing shoes and grading sole leather. Immigrant women occupied other gender-specific jobs, such as perforating and stamping, cementing and trimming, lining making, ironing, repairing, and inspecting.

Another closely related factor attracting immigrant women to factory labor was the gender segregation within the factory itself. Many firms in the early twentieth century adopted policies that gendered the organization of the workplace space and the activities performed within it. Institutionalized segregation thus served to reinforce management's respect for standards of sexual propriety in the workplace.[13]

At Endicott Johnson women worked in separate rooms at jobs designated as women's work. The stitching rooms, for example, where nearly a quarter of all Italian women worked, held several hundred women employees from different cultures working side by side.

Women applying for work at the shoe factories were often motivated to seek employment for a variety of reasons, with American-born women and foreign-born women often having different motivations. Single, young native-born rural girls often took jobs to become independent. It was an escape from isolated, rural farm life for many young women,[14] such as Katie Chopiak, who declared, "I wanted to get away from home! [My mother] didn't even want to listen to me—but then one time my father came, and . . . I told him that I wanted to go to work. So when he went back to Endicott, he took me."[15] Young women growing up in the Triple Cities took jobs early in their working lives. They often worked at the shoe factories in order to contribute to the family's income, to save money for a technical or vocational school, to become independent from their families, or even to find husbands.[16] Helen Weaver, born to a family of ten in Binghamton in 1897, was anxious to leave high school as soon as possible so she could earn her own money and become independent. Unlike immigrant girls who worked as factory operatives, Helen had obtained enough skills in high school to secure an office job at Endicott Johnson.[17]

Daughters of immigrant families sought employment at an early age almost exclusively for the purpose of contributing to the family's income. The 1925 New York State census indicates that 31 percent of all males aged 13 to 18 as well as 31 percent of all females aged 13 to 18 were gainfully employed and contributing to their family's income. Daughters of immigrant families were expected to work for the good of the family rather than for personal or individual goals. Even those young women who disliked school, dropped out, and went to work in the shoe factories remained at home and contributed a substantial amount—if not their entire pay envelope—to the family fund.[18] Family members, especially children, felt a strong sense of obligation to assist their parents. In some families, especially those with several young children, the work of daughters made it possible for mothers to remain at home. Bridgetta Bianco was typical. An Italian immigrant, she was one of twelve children who, at the age of fourteen, quit school and took a job in the shoe factories. Her labor made it possible for her mother to remain at home and take care of the younger siblings.[19] Rose Grassi was the daughter of Italian immigrant parents who had died young, leaving fifteen children behind. Rose and her eight sisters quit school in their teens and took jobs at Endicott Johnson to help sustain the family while their brothers remained in school and graduated.[20] Elisabetta Manziano, one of eight children, quit school and went to work when she was sixteen. She, too, worked for the collective good of the family. Elisabetta's immigrant father rewarded her efforts with daily lunch money and fifty cents weekly for her discretionary use.[21] Mary Monticello, who was nearing high school graduation, quit school in the twelfth grade because her family needed the money.[22]

In interviews with Italian immigrant families in New York City at the turn of the century, social worker Louise Odencrantz discovered what she called "sex differentiation" in contributions to the family budget. Working sons usually paid board (about half their earnings) and kept the remainder for their own purposes. On the other hand, she noted, "it was assumed that the daughter's pay envelope should be turned over to her mother intact."[23] Vicki Ruiz notes similar expectations in California, where Mexican American cannery operatives were young single daughters who lived at home and contributed all or part of their paychecks to the family income.[24] This pattern was evident among Endicott's Italians as well. Several interviews reveal that parents often felt that sons needed spending money, whereas daughters did not. In addition, daughters were often, although not always, expected to make sacrifices for brothers, as in the case of Rose Grassi, who proudly revealed, "Me and my sisters dropped out of school and worked in the shoe factories so that our brothers could graduate from high school."[25]

Family expectations of daughters' contributions to the welfare of the family continued throughout the years of the Depression. One Depression-era survey of Italian families in East Harlem, for example, found that one-half of the boys but the majority of girls contributed their entire earnings to the family.[26] Employment did not necessarily mean economic independence for young Italian women, but at the same time, exposure to American values often led immigrant daughters to resist parental control of their wage earnings. According to Judith Smith, daughters had a stronger sense of their own needs, peer pressure toward certain kinds of consumption, and a feeling of entitlement to their earnings.[27] In Endicott young immigrant working women, influenced by American consumerism and culture, required a little spending money to eat an occasional fifteen-cent lunch at the Endicott Johnson Restaurant with their co-workers or to purchase the latest pair of Endicott Johnson ladies' oxfords.

Both male and female children of Italian immigrants were inclined to work at Endicott Johnson either before completing high school or after graduation. Italian familial work patterns were reinforced by George F. Johnson, whose company policy was to groom the children of his employees to follow in the footsteps of their parents by entering employment at the shoe factories.

Kinship Patterns of Labor Recruitment and Childcare

The practice of familial recruitment and the creation of kinship paths into the workplace have been recognized as important conduits for immigrant employment.[28] A 1924 investigation of Italian females in New York City reported that 75 percent acquired their first jobs through friends or relatives and that these same women were ashamed to seek employment alone and would quit a job if friends or kin left.[29] Once in Endicott, Italian women working in Endicott Johnson factories obtained jobs for other family members. Mothers and fathers obtained jobs for daughters and sons; family members recruited nieces, nephews, and in-laws. Women did not have to go into the factories alone to apply for jobs but were accompanied by other family members. Sisters often worked side by side in the stitching rooms, like fourteen-year-old Frances Vivona, whose older sister helped her get a job right next to her in the stitching department, stitching tongue linings into shoes.[30] Most Italian women who became part of the Endicott Johnson workforce already had husbands, children, sisters, brothers, or other relatives employed there.

In some instances, entire families worked in the same department. In 1925, Vito Longo and his wife Maria both worked in the tanneries, performing different jobs. Vito's brother, Frank, and Frank's wife, Mary, had recently arrived from Italy and were residing in the same household with Vito and Maria. Frank and Mary obtained jobs in the tanneries through their brother and sister-in-law. This pattern was not unique to Italians. French Canadians working in the Amoskeag Mills in New England "brought their relatives to the factory, assisted in their placement and taught them industrial work processes."[31] In fact, many new workers learned their jobs from friends or relatives. This was especially important, since most immigrant women could not speak English when they entered the factories. Even with instruction and support from other women, however, some young workers never became comfortable with the machines or factory labor. One such employee shared her frustration: "I went to work on a stitching machine. I looked at the machine and five minutes later I said, 'I'm going home.' The ladies were very nice; they helped me, but I couldn't learn to do the fancy stitching."[32]

For most new workers, the presence of other family members working in the factory helped lessen the difficulty or timidity on the part of immigrant women entering factory work for the first time. They, along with experienced workers from other ethnic backgrounds, were willing to help ease the transition of greenhorns to factory life.

The practical problems of child rearing could be a formidable reason for keeping mothers from participating in wage labor. The impact of childbearing and child rearing on women's patterns of working outside the home is reflected in employment records showing that 61.2 percent of working Italian wives had no children, 15.4 percent had one child, 9.6 percent had two children, and 7.6 percent had three. The percentages continue to diminish to a maximum of nine children. These figures resemble the 1925 New York State census, where data analysis shows that 55 percent of working Italian women had no children. The data for women of all ethnic backgrounds, including native-born women, reveal decreased participation in the workforce when children were introduced as a variable in their lives. Italian figures most resemble those of Slavic women workers, for whom 69 percent of working wives had no children, while 11.1 percent had one child, 8.9 percent had two children, and 3.4 percent had three. Similarly, the percentages continue to diminish to a maximum of nine children among Slavic women as well. This reveals the practical problems that child rearing presented, inhibiting mothers from seeking wage work outside the home.

Of the 152 Endicott Johnson employment cards that stated the reason for leaving, pregnancy was the most frequent reason cited by Italian women. Other women reported they could no longer work because they were needed at home to care for their small children. A significant number of Italian women dropped out of the workforce long enough to remain at home with their children until school age, thereupon returning to the factories. Elisabetta Manziano, daughter of immigrant parents and herself the wife of an Italian immigrant, was typical: "I worked for six years at Endicott Johnson before my child was born. Then I took a three-month leave of absence and returned to work for twenty more years until I retired."[33] Rose Grassi Annis also worked for Endicott Johnson until her children were born. After her second child was in school, she returned to work, adding that she felt it was a necessity. "Besides," she said, "I enjoyed it."[34]

Working mothers were helped by Endicott Johnson's practices that permitted school-aged children to come to the factory after school and wait near their mothers' workplace until the end of the day.[35] To a certain extent, this represented familiar working patterns in rural Italy, where women brought children with them to nearby fields where they raised crops.[36]

The task of caring for children proved much more complicated in the United States than it had been in Italy, where women's economic production was closely tied to domestic functions and where young girls worked alongside women in the fields. In Endicott immigrant mothers working outside the home relied on the Italian tradition of familial support for childcare. Working women with small children resorted to widespread kinship groups within the community. Former Endicott Johnson employees recall that, while they worked, Italian women left their children with sisters, mothers, aunts, and even aging fathers. Dolores Molinaro, daughter of Bridgetta Bianco, said "my grandmother lived in an upstairs apartment and took care of me while my mother worked at Endicott Johnson."[37] Rose Grassi Annis's sister, who lived around the corner, cared for her three children during the years she worked in the shoe factory. The concentration of Italians and the tendency for Italians to live close to kin, or even in extended households with kin, provided a pool of women located within the ethnic enclave to meet the childcare needs of women workers.[38] Kinship ties made it possible for Italian women to leave their homes, secure that family members were caring for the little ones.

Proximity between Home and Work

Urban geographers have identified spatial factors as an important consideration of women contemplating wage labor outside the home. As early as 1907, pioneering studies revealed that women worked closer to home than did men,[39] and, more recently, several geographers have concluded that "women, especially married women, do not join the paid labor force unless appropriate jobs are conveniently located vis-à-vis their residence."[40] The geographic and spatial relationship between ethnic neighborhood and the factory site was a major factor contributing to Italian women's participation in industrial labor in Endicott. Studies from various cities also note the tendency of Italian women to work close to home. Louise Odencrantz, for example, concluded that location was a very important consideration for Italian women working in New York City at the turn of the century, noting that "most Italian women worked in factories within walking distance of their homes." In addition, she discovered that "the very fact that a firm had moved was sufficient excuse for leaving a position."[41] Barbara Klaczynska, finding that few Italian women worked outside their homes in Philadelphia between 1910 and 1930, reached a similar conclusion. Even though Philadelphia was primarily a textile-producing city with many sewing jobs for women, the factories were concentrated in the northeast section of the city and Italians lived in the south section, a nonindustrial area that provided few light-industry jobs for women.[42] The presence of light industry in Philadelphia was not a guarantee that Italian women would participate in wage labor, because the opportunities existed but their location limited Italian women's choices.

In Endicott 92 percent of Italian working women in the shoe factories lived near the factories, most of them on Oak Hill, Squires Street, or Bermond, O'Dell, and Hill Avenues. When these streets are plotted on a map the correlation between factory sites and the Italians' residential locations and the likelihood of immigrant women seeking employment is pronounced. These streets on the north side were only blocks away from the shoe factories, a five- to ten-minute walk at most.

Because of the geographical proximity between home and work in Endicott, Italian women walked to the factory with other women, often sisters, cousins, or neighbors. More important, they walked through residential areas, passing the homes of relatives or *paesani* from their native village in Italy. Thus, for Italian women, employment at Endicott Johnson did not place them in a threatening or vulnerable position by requiring transportation to another location, nor did it remove them from the close proximity of their homes, their children, or their ethnic neighborhoods.

Immigrant women and their daughters entered wage labor in Endicott, but, as suggested here, several factors made factory work attractive and manageable for Italian women. These factors—the division of labor and gender segregation in the workshop, kinship networks of labor recruitment and childcare, and the geographical settlement patterns of Italians in Endicott—played out in ways that were consistent with immigrant women's cultural values. The gender division of labor prominent in the shoe industry was characteristic of women's work division in Italy, whether in domestic production at home, in agricultural work in the fields, or in factory labor. Gender segregation in the factory was consistent with the division of labor in Italy as well as with the practice of gender segregation in public life. Italian women working in all-female departments in the factory, whether intentional or not, were upholding Italian social mores that defined male and female public spaces as separate and distinct. Similarly, when immigrant women and their daughters walked to work through Italian neighborhoods with other family members, they practiced another ritual that allowed for a traditional form of communal supervision of women.

Kinship patterns of labor recruitment provided immigrant women with female camaraderie as well as supervision within the factory itself. Finally, kinship patterns of childcare were particularly important because they provided working mothers with the crucial support they needed in order to be able to leave their homes for factory labor with peace of mind.

Males and females were equally concerned about the potential conflict faced by working mothers and the roles that they traditionally held as childcare providers. Most Italian husbands recognized the need for their wives to work and supplement the family income but, at the same time, agonized over the care of their children. According to Elisabetta Manziano, "most of the Italian men we knew wanted their wives to work."[43] Italian immigrant Frank Allio, who was ninety-four years old at the time of my 1987 interview with him, declared that his Italian-born wife worked at the factory before they married and continued working until she had her first child, adding that "all women worked here; women needed to work here." Mary Allio did not work after the birth of her children, however, because they had no family members in Endicott who could provide childcare.[44]

Among Italians, the tradition of having other family members, especially grandmothers, care for the children of working mothers has long been viewed as an acceptable and a desirable way for young couples to get ahead. Elisabetta Manziano said that her husband did not object to her working outside the home but, when she gave birth to their first child, he asked her to take some time off. She stayed home for three months and then returned to work, leaving their infant daughter with her mother.[45] Patterns of familial support for working mothers were repeated throughout the Italian community: Bridgetta Bianco's mother cared for her daughter while she worked, and Rose Grassi Annis's sister took care of her children during the years she was employed at Endicott Johnson.

Most couples agreed that it was preferable for women to remain at home for several months or even several years after children were born, but if economic necessity made that impossible, then women could work outside the home if they had family members available to take care of their children. Family members were considered perfectly acceptable surrogates for mothers, thus providing tacit approval for Italian women who found it necessary to work outside the home.

Endicott Johnson's Policies toward Working Mothers

Endicott Johnson's immigrant laborers found the company's program of corporate welfare consistent with Italian traditions of providing support to the extended family. Endicott Johnson's ideological concept of a "Happy Family" of workers reinforced the bonds between workers' families and the firm. This created an atmosphere that was favorable for women workers, provided direct benefits to working women, and reinforced familial goals.

The motives compelling Johnson to embark on a program of welfare capitalism were rooted in his earlier experiences as general manager of the firm, his own humble beginnings as a shoe worker, and his convictions that management has a responsibility for the well-being of its employees.

During his years as general manager of the company, Johnson committed to efforts to streamline production and increase worker efficiency. During the 1890s, Johnson came into conflict with some of the company's skilled workers who were attempting to defend both wage gains and the traditional work practices that his reforms were challenging. A reduction in skilled workers' piece rates in 1894 resulted in a strike that brought in union organizers and created a near standstill in the entire factory workforce. According to historian Gerald Zahavi, while the strike was short-lived, it strengthened Johnson's resolve that he would not tolerate a union that either challenged his authority in the factory or threatened to destroy the firm's reputation.[46]

At the same time, however, Johnson's own humble beginnings as a shoe worker at the age of thirteen in Massachusetts made him acutely aware of the economic and social plight of the working class. Having experienced the reactions of his workers to his factory reforms, particularly workers whom he respected, he came to reconsider the responsibility of management to its employees.[47] This experience may have been the most important in his resolve that the "employer is the natural labor leader."

Like many other industrialists wakened to the sentiment of Progressive Era reform, Johnson exhibited characteristics of a man motivated by a genuine spirit of goodwill toward his workers. He had been deeply influenced by the Social Gospel Movement and believed that Christians must apply the golden rule in their relations with employees. These convictions may have been strengthened by Johnson's religious conversion under evangelist Dwight L. Moody.[48]

In his efforts to institute corporate welfare at Endicott Johnson, George F. Johnson sent his son, George, and his brother, Harry, to study management-worker relationships at the Ford Company in 1917. Harry reported that he was most impressed that "Mr. Ford decided that $5.00 a day was as low a wage as a man might be expected to live on." However, Harry sensed that something was missing at Ford. The difference, he thought, was the personal contact that Endicott Johnson forged between company and workers. He noted that "the interest in the working men on the part of the Ford Company is unmistakable." However, "Mr. Ford does not live with the people—he goes into the works, but seldom—they do not know him personally—it is all handed down to them through the medium of a lot of hired people."[49]

Part of George F. Johnson's appeal was the element of personal interaction. Employees were impressed at the interest he showed in their jobs and in their personal lives. Anna Gimmie recalled that after starting work at Endicott Johnson as a young girl, Johnson walked through the factory one day. When he saw her, he said, "You have them so young in here?" And then he asked Anna her name. Anna later recalled, "You know, he remembered my name, honest, every time he would go by and say, 'Hi Anna, how ya doin?'"[50]

Workers were encouraged to approach Johnson's office to discuss a problem or just drop in and say hello. If workers felt they were being abused by a foreman or superintendent or had any complaint, "he or she was invited," not permitted, "to go to the head of the concern and state that grievance."[51]

Often, Johnson would intercede on behalf of workers or personally extend financial aid when needed. Italian employees felt they could approach Johnson for assistance, particularly in times of family crisis. For example, Mary Vallone's father, an Italian immigrant and Endicott Johnson employee, could not continue working at the factory when his wife became seriously ill and unable to take care of her four young children. Gaetano Vallone returned to work after Johnson provided day care for his children for two months, at which time their mother recovered and returned home.[52] Another Italian employee, Sam Salvatore, requested Johnson's financial help in covering burial expenses for his deceased mother-in-law. The next day Salvatore learned that the funeral director had received a check from Johnson covering the entire cost of the funeral.[53] When Bridgetta Bianco became seriously ill with a rare spleen disease, she asked the company to provide her with outside consultation. Endicott Johnson sent her to Massachusetts General Hospital and covered all the expenses.[54]

In a provocative examination of the corporation as family, Nikki Mandell reveals how advocates of welfare capitalism used the nineteenth-century Victorian family as the model for harmonious partnership between management and workers. Within the corporate family, "employers assumed the authoritative role of fathers and assigned the subordinate role of children to their employees."[55] This was precisely the model emulated by George F. Johnson, who perpetuated the idea of the company (management and workers) as a family and himself as the father. According to employee Antoinette Santodonato Sacco, "They [Endicott Johnson] would give inspiring speeches [where] they would extol the family, the workers, and the company."[56] George F. Johnson purposely cultivated his fatherly image for similar reasons. A company marching song included the line, "George F. is the daddy of this family," and Johnson made a point of personally visiting the ethnic neighborhoods where his employees lived. In a 1923 letter to a friend, he wrote, "As I go among my foreign neighbors, I am their 'Father'—even to some of the older men and women."[57]

A coherent and structured program of welfare capitalism began to evolve at Endicott Johnson after 1900. An ever-growing workforce, a geographically expanding business, the growing numbers of women workers, and the social and labor conditions that accompanied the First World War contributed significantly to its development. Like a family, corporate welfare at Endicott Johnson reinforced the bonds between management and workers.

Home of the "Square Deal"

What I am trying to do is to create confidence in the minds of the
plain workers. They have been and their ancestors have been, since
time immemorial, exploited to create wealth for others. . . . I honestly
think we have started a real "Industrial Democracy" down here . . . a
most happy and prosperous community.

—George F. Johnson, February 1923

The year 1920 found comprehensive welfare work being practiced in many
of the largest, most prominent industrial and mercantile establishments in
the country. There were many variations in welfare work, ranging from im-
proving the physical working conditions in the factories to the organization
of team sports and recreational facilities. In some companies, welfare capitalism included numerous features in the areas of employee organization, management structures in dealing with labor, wage determination, and hours of
work.[58] Programs varied from industry to industry and from business to
business, based on size, location, and resources available to employers for
investing in such programs.

Between 1916 and 1921 George F. Johnson created a program of corporate
welfare that included promoting health and safety at the workplace; providing for the needs of the family through medical benefits, health care, and
housing; and offering a variety of recreational and social activities to employees.

New employees beginning work at Endicott Johnson received a pamphlet
titled "An E-J Worker's First Lesson in the Square Deal." Workers were promised medical and health services but, as part of the "deal," Endicott Johnson
expected a "fair return, an honest effort to do the work well, and a fair and
sufficient amount of it."[59] Fundamental to this contractual agreement was
labor loyalty. As Mandell describes it, "A good welfare program would create
an environment in which workers and employers could understand their
common interest and act in partnership for their mutual benefit."[60]

Endicott Johnson's Medical Service for "the industrial worker and his
family" outlined the recently developed program:

Three separate communities are each supplied with a medical center, each
maintaining a general office for diagnosis and treatment, and each maintaining hospital beds for the care of maternity cases.

Any worker sustaining an industrial accident—no matter how trivial or
how severe—is immediately directed to one of the three medical stations for
treatment. In addition to providing medical care . . . the injured employee

receives full pay for his loss of time from the beginning of any industrial accident.[61]

The corporation's medical service included physicians, dentists, dental hygienists, physical therapists, nurses, bacteriologists, pharmacists, and technicians. Endicott Johnson built hospitals and medical centers in Binghamton, Johnson City, and Endicott with specialties for ear, nose, and throat disorders. A convalescent home was built at a nearby farm, and two tubercular asylums were established in Saranac, New York. The company provided a staff of visiting nurses who provided follow-up work to injured or ill workers and their families. In addition, Endicott Johnson provided workers' compensation, old age and widows' pensions, sickness relief, burial funds, and housekeeping assistance.[62]

In the early months of 1929, a study carried out by a doctor appointed by President Hoover's commission to study industrial medicine found "nothing in industrial medicine [that] could compare with Endicott Johnson service."[63]

Gender and Welfare Work

By the mid-1920s, Endicott Johnson had created a model of welfare work in industry with impressive and progressive services for women and children. An Endicott Johnson employee or the wife of an employee could receive prenatal and postnatal care at a company clinic and deliver her baby at an Endicott Johnson maternity hospital.

Employment at Endicott Johnson provided women with an opportunity to take advantage of the firm's many welfare services. One female employee stated, "I was determined to get to E-J's no matter how, because I could get benefits. . . . I thought, well, if I don't make high wages, so what? I'll get the benefits, and I'll be better off."[64]

Increased female employment at Endicott Johnson was a reflection of trends taking place nationwide. As more and more women entered the paid labor force, economic, political, and social concerns encouraged the feminization of welfare work.

The feminization of welfare work was, to a great extent, a concern of employers with their public image. Concern over the female role in the family and the social cost of women's wage work was an issue that loomed large in early twentieth-century America. Economic necessity drove women into the workforce, but women workers had high turnover rates and were more likely to leave jobs than men. Mandell concludes that welfare work directed at women had a twofold purpose. It sought to inculcate middle-class habits that would make women more industrious and loyal workers, and it assumed a fundamental responsibility to teach female workers to be good housewives and mothers.[65]

At Endicott Johnson, welfare policies directed at working women included the establishment of the Ideal Training School by Mary Johnson (George F.'s wife) in 1917, for the purpose of instructing immigrant wives and their children in good housekeeping and in cooking wholesome "American meals." Sewing classes instructed women and girls how to select materials and make their own clothing, while classes were also offered in decorating and furnishing a house. Over 700 children and 267 mothers and employed women attended classes by 1935. Established by Johnson's management in 1918, the Little Mother's League was geared primarily toward the daughters of Endicott Johnson working mothers. Similar to the objectives of the Ideal Training School, girls were taught how to prepare food, keep the home clean, and, most important, how to care for younger children at home. They were even taught the principles of home sanitation and the rules and regulations governing the collection of garbage.[66] Aimed at helping young girls who cared for the house and younger siblings while both parents were at work, it also served as a way to inculcate American middle-class values of morality and working habits to immigrants and their children.[67]

While the corporation never progressed far enough to provide childcare facilities, it did respond to the individual requests of working mothers. Former Endicott Johnson employees cited the crucial importance of the corporation's allowance of flexible hours for working mothers. Though they were not paid for time lost from work, women were allowed to leave work whenever their children were ill. Mothers reported that they generally took a week off when their children were sick with childhood diseases.[68] And, as mentioned above, women with school-aged children were permitted to have their children come to the factory after school and wait near their mother's workplace until the end of the day.

In July 1923, Endicott Johnson began sponsored summer activities at playgrounds in Endicott and Johnson City especially designed for the children of working women. This was a result of pressure brought on the company by working mothers in the ethnic neighborhoods of Endicott. In 1919, Endicott Johnson built a playground on the north side of Endicott. That occasion prompted a special request from immigrant mothers. Several women contacted Endicott Johnson, asking "if we could not have a day nursery on the kiddies playground with someone interested in children and capable of looking after the little ones brought there by mothers who must work during the day?"[69] The company responded to the mothers' request in July 1923 with a program of summer activities at playgrounds in both Endicott and Johnson City for the children of working mothers. During the summer months, children spent time playing, eating, and sleeping under regulated conditions in what Endicott Johnson referred to as a "day nursery."[70]

Requests to the company for day care reflect a considerable amount of assertiveness among the immigrant working women on the north side of Endicott. Made up primarily of Italians, Poles, Czechs, and Russians, the north side of Endicott was a polyglot of ethnic enclaves inhabited by working women who were increasingly coming to terms with the burdens and conflicts of marriage, family, and work. In doing so, they were beginning to make specific demands on their place of employment and their community. In the process, Italian women were becoming activists in transforming the workplace to meet the demands of working wives and mothers. At the same time, Endicott Johnson was helping to preserve the sanctity of motherhood by helping working mothers with the difficulties of childcare.

"Better Homes for Less Money"

Johnson sought to create an ideal industrial community, with factories surrounded by homes for workers, parks, and playgrounds. In addition to promoting close ties between working-class families and the company, homebuilding in Johnson's mind was also the answer to numerous social and industrial ills. "There can be no security," Johnson said, "there can be no guarantee of prosperity and industrial peace except through homes owned by the plain citizen."[71] Johnson, like many other employers, viewed property ownership as an important way of reorienting workers' values. One industrial expert observed that "men are more likely to be sober, steady, industrious, and faithful if they own their own visible property."[72]

During the 1920s alone, the company built close to five thousand homes in Endicott and Johnson City and sold them to workers at cost. To pay for the homes, the company deducted money each week from a worker's paycheck. Former Endicott Mayor Marian Corino, who grew up in an Endicott Johnson house, remarked that "the home building program enabled many immigrant workers, like my parents and grandparents, to realize their dream of owning a piece of property."[73] The need to provide decent housing led

Endicott Johnson to establish a program that would become one of the most popular with its workers.

During the early years of the company's expansion into Endicott, even before the homebuilding program began, workers could buy land from the Endicott Johnson Realty Company. Instead of waiting for an Endicott Johnson home to be built, Johnson would often aid his employees by providing them with gifts of money and bank loans to help them build their own homes.[74] In 1916 and 1917, for example, at least fifty-six lots were bought by Italians in Endicott.[75] Endicott Johnson houses were built with six or seven rooms and every modern convenience and sold at from $2,500 to $4,000 each.[76] Compared to Pullman's planned community, for example, Endicott Johnson's design for workers' homes was far superior. About two-thirds of Pullman's families lived in buildings with multiple apartments. Only one-third lived in single-family homes, containing five rooms and a basement, which were rented primarily by skilled workingmen. Furthermore, Pullman's practice of renting homes to workers never gave them the opportunity to gain a stake in the community through home ownership.

Endicott Johnson's homes were built on generous lots, and plenty of space was available for a garden and a garage if so desired. To reduce the possible negative association of Endicott Johnson homes with company houses, the design of each home varied. Exteriors were finished off in clapboard, cedar shingles, and/or stucco, while the interiors reflected design qualities of a cozy bungalow. The streets and sidewalks were broad and well paved, and thousands of trees were planted along the curbs and on the lawns, with hedges or Japanese shrubs.

Homes built by Endicott Johnson were very popular with Italian workers. An analysis of 285 existing records of immigrants and second-generation Italian families who purchased Endicott Johnson homes in Endicott during the 1920s and 1930s reflects Johnson's policy of providing homes to "large families who need it the most."[77] For example, Anna and Fred Corino, the immigrant parents of twelve children, purchased a home in 1920, and Angelo and Filomena Grassi, parents of fifteen children, bought their Endicott Johnson home in 1928, only four years after Angelo began working for the company.[78]

Homebuilding continued throughout the 1930s and 1940s, but could hardly keep up with the demand. In a letter dated 1935, Johnson's brother, the homebuilding supervisor, reported that the houses were coming along very well. "They are far from finished in every respect," he added, "but people are just so hard up for shelter that they are willing to move into anything. So just as quick as we can get a house into any kind of shape we let families in, with the understanding we will complete them as rapidly as possible."[79]

While Endicott Johnson's home ownership policy was aimed at providing low-cost housing for Endicott Johnson "working men and their families," Endicott Johnson working women were also eligible to purchase homes. For Mary Simona, an Italian immigrant and widow with four children, the opportunity to purchase her own home would have been out of the question were it not for Endicott Johnson's home-ownership program. Mary was a steady worker and had been employed in the tanneries for over sixteen years. Ten years after the death of her husband, she became a home owner. In 1921, her picture accompanied an article in the *E-J Workers Review,* pointing out that "her work in the Upper Leather tannery enables her to support them [her four children] nicely."[80] According to Endicott Johnson Realty records, many Italian women independently purchased homes between 1918 and 1941.[81] In addition to those women who independently purchased homes, 58 female Endicott Johnson employees (20 percent of the 285 Italian families for whom we have records), along with their spouses, purchased Endicott Johnson homes.[82] Lena Sementelli (and her husband, Dom), who began working at Endicott Johnson in 1923, purchased a company-built home after the birth of her fifth child. Lena retired from Endicott Johnson at the age of 65, after thirty-nine years of employment. Regina Segre, who started working for the corporation in 1915 at the age of fifteen, realized her dream of home ownership in the early 1930s, when she, her husband, and their five children moved into a newly built Endicott Johnson home.[83]

Of all the benefits provided employees by Endicott Johnson, owning a home built by Endicott Johnson was perhaps the most appealing to Italian immigrants. Home ownership was a primary goal of those Italian families who were committed to remaining in America. Studies of social mobility in several communities have placed considerable emphasis on the role of home ownership. John Bodnar, Roger Simon, and Michael Weber, in their study of immigrant groups in Pittsburgh, argue that home ownership represented a major form of success. For Poles and Italians, "homeowning and the creation of stable neighborhoods were clearly high priorities. In addition to providing a sense of status, it gave the owners greater control over their environment, provided a form of enforced savings with a resultant equity, and had the potential of providing a source of income."[84] In Buffalo, Virginia Yans writes, "Italians had their own standard of achievement, namely, the acquisition of family property, usually a home." In fact, she added, "thousands of Italians had become home owners, often sacrificing their children's education and career prospects to do so."[85] For many Italians, the purchase of a home was the main achievement for which many sacrifices were often made, yet, the sacrifices made by those Italians employed at Endicott Johnson were perhaps not as great as those made by Italians elsewhere, thanks to Endicott Johnson's liberal purchasing arrangements. Down payments were low, if required at all; mortgaging was financed through a bank controlled by Endicott Johnson; and, finally, home prices were as low as possible, only a small percentage over the cost of building them.

It was crucial that home owners meet their end of the contract by making payments on time and taking care of their homes. According to George F. Johnson, the "eligible, or desirable worker is one who hasn't any debt, who is ready, willing and able to meet his obligations, and to secure (with an opportunity and a good chance to pay for) a home for himself."[86] Endicott Johnson homes were offered on very liberal terms, with flexible payment schedules allowed during periods of slack work, particularly during recessions or depressions. In addition, easy credit terms and flexible payments in time of financial duress gave workers an opportunity to buy a home when they might otherwise not have been able to do so. Even with the best intentions, however, workers could fall behind on their mortgages. Many immigrant families experienced hard times and occasionally could not make their house payments. When this occurred, family members, usually wives, went to the Endicott Johnson Personnel Office and asked for help. The company allowed employees to make their payments when they were able to do so. When Elisabetta Manziano was home on maternity leave she approached the company and asked for financial help. They helped pay her heat, electricity, and mortgage while she was out of work.[87] Another worker recalled that "they [Endicott Johnson] paid your taxes; they paid everything. You didn't have any other payments, just that. If you needed money, you went to the Sales Building and told them that you needed some of what you had paid, [that] you wasn't [sic] able to pay that month and they would give it back to you. They'd give you so much of it if you wanted the whole thing or if you wanted just part of it."[88]

Employment at Endicott Johnson appeared even more attractive to Italian workers, who viewed home ownership as an important indicator of success. That Italians just happened to purchase homes nearest to the factories suggests that it may not have been coincidental at all, rather a conscious decision made by immigrant families for whom work outside the home was the norm for women.

Welfare Capitalism and Italian Workers

Business and labor historians have argued employer's motives and workers' responses to welfare capitalism. In a pioneering study of American labor in the 1920s and 1930s, Irving Bernstein argued that the central purpose of welfare work was avoidance of trade unionism.[89] Gerald Zahavi argues that Endicott Johnson's practices—such as medical services, homebuilding, and company recreational programs—were created to forestall labor conflict, improve worker morale, and promote employee loyalty.[90] In addition to Zahavi, other labor historians such as Stephen Meyers and Lizabeth Cohen generally agree that welfare capitalism was a form of labor control and antiunion strategy but one that permitted workers' creative transformation of policies and practices. In a more recent study of business and benevolence, Andrea Tone affirms that "employers eager to check and repel the tide of government regulation proffered welfare capitalism as an alternative to welfare statism."[91]

Cooperation, industrial harmony, and labor loyalty were at the heart of George F. Johnson's policies of cultivating close ties between working-class families and the corporation. It is clear from Italian employees that the company's policies and George F. Johnson, in particular, were relatively effective in winning labor loyalty from workers.

What was the effect of Endicott Johnson's program of corporate welfare on Italian workers? Luciano Iorizzo and Salvatore Mondello's examination of *padroni* and Italian workers in New York State reveals that *padroni* existed in virtually every upstate New York community with a substantial Italian population except one—Endicott. Why? The authors believe it was due to the "benevolent paternalism of George F. Johnson." They suggest that he "provided the kinds of services for his foreign-born workers that they usually could obtain only from their own leaders."[92] In many ways Johnson may be viewed as a kind of *padrone* to his Italian employees without the usual negative connotations associated with the term. The Italians in Johnson's employ sought help from him much the same way that Italians of southern Italy sought the protection and aid of a local benefactor, whom they believed was the only one who could take care of their needs.

Johnson held a special place among immigrants and second-generation Italians who worked for him. When asked what she thought about Johnson and his policies, Frances Vivona Cizanek replied, "He was our Santa Claus."[93] Elisabetta Manziano, who was helped out by Endicott Johnson during some financial difficulties, remarked, "George F. was like a father to us. He was a peach of a man—you could talk to him anytime."[94] According to Mary Monticello, "We were very loyal to Endicott Johnson. They were good to us." Her husband, Fred, added, "We didn't make a lot of money, but we were the happiest workers in the world."[95]

The goals of Endicott Johnson's corporate welfare program were strikingly similar to those described by Tamara Hareven and Randolph Langenback in their study of the Amoskeag Company in Manchester, New Hampshire. Both companies instituted paternalistic measures devised to "attract additional immigrants to the city, to socialize them to industrial work, to instill loyalty to the Company, to curb labor unrest, and to prevent unionization."[96] But Endicott never became a company town like Amoskeag, nor did it evolve into a Southern-style mill village. While it was the largest employer in Endicott and dominated the industrial landscape of the Triple Cities, Endicott Johnson never became a company that owned and controlled everything, including employees.

Loyalty in return for the benefits and protection provided by George F. Johnson was a familiar concept to Italians emigrating from a country where social interactions were based on patronage. The policies of welfare capitalism at the company provided flexibility in hours and conditions for working mothers, medical benefits, and assistance in home buying—benefits that were critical for women who took seriously their roles and responsibilities in the family. If economic necessity pushed Italian women in Endicott into the workforce, they were simultaneously pulled by an industry that provided family benefits.

And yet, all of this is not to say that Endicott Johnson workers were always contented workers. Most of the women employed at Endicott Johnson were stitchers, operating sewing machines and stitching together the uppers and linings of boots and shoes. Stitching-room jobs were routine and repetitive. On most stitching jobs the workers placed small leather pieces in a certain position, ran them through the machine, and removed the finished piece. Some performed more specialized tasks, such as fine topstitching. The work process in the factories was organized so that one worker performed a single step in the production process over and over again. The routine and tedious nature of their work led many women to change jobs frequently.

While there was much sociability among the immigrant women who worked in the factories, there was also a strong sense of competition. The stitching rooms, as well as most other departments at Endicott Johnson, were dominated by piece-wage that led to competition among workers. This meant that the pace of work was, to some extent, under the control of each worker, but it also meant that the rate at which each did her work could be measured. The wage payment system was designed to ensure that each employee worked at the fastest possible pace. Piece rates paid workers a certain price for performing their particular operation on a dozen shoes. When a worker finished a case of shoes, she clipped a small coupon off the bottom of the printed routing slip. The number of coupons turned in at the end of the week, multiplied by the rate for the job, determined the amount she was paid. The more they produced, the more money they made.[97] At Endicott Johnson, the competition among female piece wage earners became fierce. Italian women in particular were known to work excessively in order to hand in the most coupons at the end of the day. A former employee revealed that in the 1920s, Italian women were referred to as "grabbers," a term used to describe those women who "grabbed" others' work when backs were turned so they could accumulate more coupons. One former employee remarked that "Italian women worked like their lives depended on it."[98]

There were other times, however, when women worked collectively. Workers often cooperated to protect themselves against rate cutting. They realized that if some of them earned more money than the managers wanted to pay, the rate for the job would be cut and they would all have to work faster to earn the same wages as before. In many workrooms, they held production down to a safe level and tried to outwit the foremen and others who set the rates. Workers also acted collectively when attempting to negotiate with management. They even conducted shop-floor strikes to enforce their demands. While the workers were rarely granted the increased rates they sought, their actions did make a difference; management thought twice before imposing wage cuts. Endicott Johnson officials knew that there were limits to what the workers would accept.[99] For example, Bridgetta Bianco led a walkout made up of her fellow Slavic and Italian co-workers. The women presented a collective grievance to the company against working conditions, refusing to return to their machines until their demands were met. They won.[100] As Patricia Pessar illustrates in her study of Dominican working women in the United States, working-class family values were transformed within the workplace into concrete collective actions for improvements in wages and work options.[101]

Endicott Johnson's labor policies were based on the belief that managers and workers could resolve their differences without the involvement of outsiders. According to Zahavi, the corporation faced the first of a series of formidable challenges to its paternalistic policies in the 1930s. The union promised to pursue wage increases, job protection, overtime pay, and equalization of work. In response, the company issued appeals urging its workers to ignore the "strangers" in their midst and to remain loyal to the corporation. The compact between management and labor, the "Square Deal," rested on the premise that grievances and conflicts would be resolved without the involvement of intermediaries. A union presence within the corporation, managers reminded the workers, threatened the very foundations of the "Happy Family."[102]

Loyalty to Endicott Johnson prohibited Italian women from joining a union. Mary Monticello felt that joining a union would be a betrayal to the company whom she "felt had been good to them."[103] Elisabetta Manziano reported that "people felt they didn't need a union," but she quietly added that "'George F.' would come right in the factory and try to discourage them from a union."[104] Dolores Bianco Wood said that "workers were afraid to join a union, they were afraid they would lose their jobs."[105] "E-J didn't want a union," according to Frances Vivona Cizanek, "so most of them [workers] went along with it because they were unsure of how a union would be."[106]

The threat of unionization at Endicott Johnson launched resistance among loyal workers and local businessmen. The Triple Cities Civic and Workers' Committee (an antiunion organization) received the support of community religious and ethnic associations, including the Sons of Italy, St. Anthony of Padua Church, Holy Name Society, and the St. Sebastian Club, among others.[107]

For women workers in particular, the welfare services, especially the medical benefits that Endicott Johnson provided, outweighed the low wages they received. The fear that benefits would be retracted was reason enough for many workers to become antiunion. In 1939, when the votes were cast, 80 percent of all voting employees voted to keep unions out. Even through the most difficult years of the Depression, welfare capitalism remained preferable to unionism for Endicott Johnson workers.[108] Welfare capitalism had weakened the attraction of unions to Endicott Johnson employees and kept workers loyal to the company.

Immigrant women's culture, leisure, and behavior could be severely limited because of lack of access to public life, particularly if they were married. Employment outside the home, however, expanded the notion of women's place. As wage earners, Italian women had access to social organizations, leisure, and a voice outside the domestic sphere.

As factory workers, Italian women were exposed to a culture defined by the shop floor. Women freely admitted that they enjoyed the social life accompanying work at Endicott Johnson. Their co-workers became their friends after

working hours, and their social life evolved around company parties and pic-
nics. Working at Endicott Johnson provided more than just a pay envelope for
women. The commingling with other women at work created a sense of be-
longing to a community. Tamara Hareven writes of the importance of friend-
ships that emerged among workers in factories and mills. At Amoskeag, friend-
ships "often lasted a lifetime and would frequently overlap kinship ties."[109] In
the South, Jacqueline Dowd Hall learned that mill villages were much more
than a place to work and earn a living. They were the setting in which men
and women fell in love, married, reared their children, and retired in old age.[110]
The same was true at Endicott Johnson. In oral interviews, former workers
acknowledged the relationships that emerged and endured among co-workers
long after their working days were over.

On the shop floor, young women discussed strategies for meeting available
men, while older women commiserated over husbands and children. Marital status was reflected in lunchtime activities, as married women remained
close to their machines, eating a sandwich from home, while single women
headed for the factory lunchrooms, where by chance, they might meet a
young man working in another department.[111]

In her study of working women and leisure in New York City at the turn
of the century, Kathy Peiss indicates that "women's notions of leisure were
reaffirmed through their positive social interactions within the workplace."[112]
There is much evidence for this at Endicott Johnson.

Women's life cycle often shaped the ways in which women experienced
leisure. Married Italian-born workers participated in activities largely centered on family outings. Workers and their families enjoyed picnicking in
company-built parks, boating, and attending band concerts, company pa-
rades, and carnivals. Young single immigrant women, along with second-
generation Italian Americans, moreover, became active participants in sports
and recreational activities by joining company glee clubs, performing in
theatrical productions, and ice-skating at Endicott Johnson skating rinks.[113]
A 1920 article in the *E-J Workers Review* featured Susie Signoriella and Hel-
en Venturino,[114] two young Italian immigrant workers. The women had just
participated in a Columbus Day celebration sponsored by Endicott Johnson.
Signoriella was attired as "America," while Venturino represented their native land, Italy. "Italy" was pictured in the *Review* clasping hands in hearty
friendship with "America."[115]

Endicott Johnson offered Italian female wage laborers an arena for creating and expanding their roles in the New World.

Reassessing Italian Women's Participation in Wage Labor

Immigrant women, drawing from premigration work patterns that supported female contributions to the family economy, continued contributing to the family economy in the United States, albeit in new and different ways. In Endicott Italian women, married and single, as well as their daughters, left their homes for wage labor. The case of Endicott is significant because it reveals that, when the right conditions existed, married Italian women did participate in wage labor outside the home.

The factors encouraging Italian women to seek out certain kinds of occupations while excluding them from others has been at the center of an ongoing scholarly debate for over two decades. The argument that culturally enforced male opposition (indicative of an especially oppressive Italian patriarchy) kept Italian women out of the workforce[116] is seriously questioned by the work histories of Italian women in Endicott.[117] A major difference accounting for the participation of Italian women in wage labor in Endicott compared to the low participation of women in wage labor in Yans's study of Buffalo, New York, for example, rests in the nature of the industrial structure of these two cities. Endicott was a city of light industry, providing jobs for women. A high correlation between light industry and women's participation rates in wage labor was noted in a 1927 survey conducted in neighboring Binghamton by Nelle Swartz, director for the Bureau of Women in Industry. Swartz's study revealed that the proportion of married women working in Binghamton's industries (shoe and cigar manufacturing) was more than twice as high compared to other cities in the United States with a similar population. Other New York State cities with comparable populations and significant numbers of married women workers were Utica (24 percent) and Amsterdam (34 percent), cities that were also dominated by light industry, particularly textiles.[118]

Buffalo, on the other hand, was characterized by heavy industry—pig iron and steel production; metals and machinery; brass, copper, and aluminum production; machinery and electrical appliances; automobiles; railroad equipment; and chemical and oil products—sectors offering few employment opportunities for women. Only 9 percent of all married women were employed outside the home in Buffalo in 1920.[119] The industrial structure of Buffalo was in fact similar to the industrial structure of Milwaukee, which also had few Italian women working outside the home.

Italian women embraced new employment opportunities and expanded their roles in America and did so within a largely Italian social and cultural milieu. This is evident by the kinship networks recruiting women into the factories, the gender segregation of the workforce, the kinship networks that provided day care for working mothers, and the geographical settlement patterns creating proximity of home to workplace.

Italian women were not docile workers. First- and second-generation Italian women were competitive laborers who requested aid and support from the company, including childcare assistance during the summer when children were home from school. Nor were they self-sacrificing mothers who worked only for the good of the family. Employment at Endicott Johnson guaranteed medical and dental care for themselves as well as their children and, for many immigrants, the acquisition of a new home. Endicott Johnson's ideological concept of a "Happy Family" of workers reinforced the bonds between workers' families and the firm. This created an atmosphere that was favorable for women workers, provided direct benefits for working women, and reinforced familial goals and values.

Italian women assessed the opportunities and benefits that Endicott Johnson offered and pursued their own goals in a company that designed policies favorable to working wives and mothers.

Women at work in the stitching department, Endicott Johnson Corporation. Courtesy of the George F. Johnson Papers, Special Collections Research Center, Syracuse University Library.

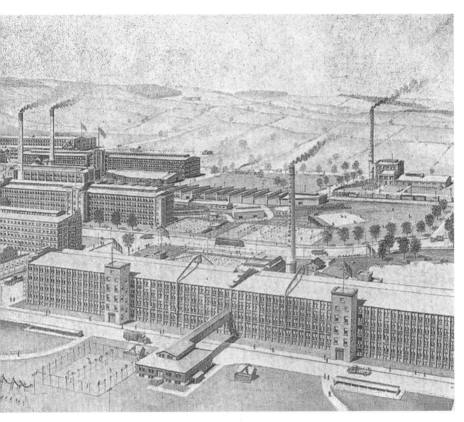

Endicott Johnson Factories and Tanneries. *A Family Affair: 8 Hour Day. Parade and Celebration by Endicott Johnson's Big Family,* 28 October 1916.

Italian women were among those who belonged to the North Side Ladies Progressive Society. *E-J Workers Review.* Courtesy of George F. Johnson Papers, Special Collections Research Center, Syracuse University Library.

Employees Susie Signoriella attired as "America" and Helen Venturino representing their native land, "Italy," in a 1920 Columbus Day celebration sponsored by Endicott Johnson. Courtesy of George F. Johnson Papers, Special Collections Research Center, Syracuse University Library.

Front cover of employees' magazine, *E-J Workers Review*, October 1920, celebrating the ethnic diversity of the Endicott Johnson workforce. Courtesy of George F. Johnson Papers, Special Collections Research Center, Syracuse University Library.

Chocolate Dipping
Candy Factory

Italian women labored in poor conditions in candy factories, working from fifty-four to sixty hours per week. Chocolate dipping candy factory, Milwaukee, Wisconsin. Courtesy of Milwaukee County Historical Society.

In 1910, Malvine Pastorino was the first professionally trained Italian American nurse in Milwaukee. Courtesy of Mario Carini, Italian Community Center, Milwaukee.

Family-owned grocery stores linked home and workplace. Italian immigrant women operate this well-stocked Milwaukee grocery store in 1930. Courtesy of Mario Carini, Italian Community Center, Milwaukee.

After studying at the University of Palermo, Sicily, Rosa Sperandandio applied for a state license from the Board of Medical Examiners to practice midwifery in Wisconsin, 21 December 1909. Courtesy of Wisconsin Historical Society (WHi-26571).

Margherita Valeri Ciotti received her diploma in 1915 from the University of Camerino, Naples, and applied for a midwifery license from the Wisconsin Board of Medical Examiners on 20 December 1923. Courtesy of Wisconsin Historical Society (WHi-26572).

3

Gender, Economic Opportunities, and Italian Businesswomen in Milwaukee

IN 1889, Mary Serio, a Sicilian immigrant, arrived in Milwaukee and settled in the Third Ward of the City. The wife of a fruit dealer, Mary ran a grocery store while raising her large family of nine children. Similarly, Stefana Balistreri, a Sicilian immigrant mother of eight, earned extra money by taking in boarders but also prepared meals for her husband's saloon and operated a grocery store in her home. Mary and Stefana created opportunities to earn an income while remaining at home by adjusting their work lives to domestic responsibilities. Their work experiences reflect a second model of immigrant women's adjustment to the urban/industrial environment.

Within a decade of settlement, the Italians of the Third Ward had established one of the most homogeneous ethnic communities in the city. By 1910 there was an ethnic parish, a public school, and diverse businesses in one of the most important business and trade centers in Milwaukee. Though close-knit and self-sustaining, the first-generation residents of the Third Ward endured many hardships. Whether they worked indoors or outdoors, the great majority of jobs taken by newly arrived Italian men were unhealthy and often dangerous. Scores of workers died from pneumonia, bronchitis, and a variety of toxic diseases. Still greater numbers developed chronic aliments, as did Mariano Carini, who worked on the coal docks, developed black lung disease, and died at the age of 42. Reports of industrial accidents filed by the city's emergency rooms provide gruesome pictures of Italian immigrants killed or maimed on the job. The most frequent and worst of the disabling accidents involved workers employed on railroads, on coal docks, and in foundries.[1]

Economic pressures added to the hardships faced by first-generation Italians in Milwaukee. Large numbers of Italian men were unskilled and worked in seasonal jobs that paid extremely low wages. For a family of eight, it was not unusual to pay $144 in rent and $370 for groceries, from an average male's annual income of $400, in 1915.[2] These circumstances created a desperate need for multiple wage earners in Italian immigrant families. Immigrants desired much more than just making ends meet, however. In America their goals included home ownership and greater opportunities for their children.

Unlike the employees of Endicott Johnson, who often realized home ownership with the financial aid of George F. Johnson and Endicott Johnson's homebuilding policies, Italians in Milwaukee had to struggle to move out of the multiple-dwelling houses they settled in following their arrival in the Third Ward. Italians had moved into an area that was seriously deteriorating, yet paid inflated prices to landlords for substandard rental units. A housing survey published in 1911 identified the Third Ward as one of ten wards in the city in which housing conditions were a menace to health and morals.[3]

Immigrant women created income-earning opportunities to help their families escape poverty and achieve familial goals, but in this Midwestern city Italian women's work experiences were dramatically different from those of Italian women in Endicott. Of the immigrant generation in Milwaukee, few Italian women worked in factories. In fact, Milwaukee boasted few light industries that might employ women. During the years of Italian community formation in Milwaukee, most of the city's labor force was employed in heavy industry, while light manufacturing represented only 32 percent of all industrial establishments.[4] Unlike Endicott, with its rich job opportunities for women in light industry, Milwaukee's heavy industries created a great demand for male labor, with few industries that generated paid employment for females.

A report by the Dillingham Commission reveals the correlation between a city's industrial makeup and the economic opportunities for immigrant workingwomen. In Philadelphia, Chicago, Boston, and New York, cities with extensive garment industries in 1900, significant numbers of Italian women, both single and married, worked outside the home. But Milwaukee, Cleveland, and Buffalo—cities dominated by steel and aluminum, breweries, oil refineries, and transportation—offered few jobs for women.[5]

In 1900, when Milwaukee's Italian community was just beginning to develop, few foreign-born women there worked outside the home. A study published by the Wisconsin Bureau of Labor noted, "In spite of the large foreign-born population of Wisconsin, 82.58% of all working women [in 1900] were native born."[6] It is not surprising that Germans made up the greatest proportion of those immigrant women working outside the home in Milwaukee at the turn of the century. They were representative of the immigrant group that had been in Milwaukee the longest, but moreover, Germans owned the majority of establishments providing employment opportunities. Of the women employed in Milwaukee's breweries, for example, only Germans were represented. German women also dominated the female labor force in Milwaukee's power laundries.[7]

The participation of ethnic women in wage labor increased dramatically by 1920, when the census reported that 56 percent of all working-women were of foreign parentage and 16 percent were foreign-born (72 percent of all women workers).[8] Though few immigrant wives worked outside the home during the early years of Italian settlement, their numbers gradually increased over time. Work patterns reveal that those Italian women who did work outside the home were either single or young married women with no children. Married women with children, but no relatives or neighbors to care for them, simply had to find other means of earning an income. In Milwaukee Italian women earning wages outside the home usually quit the labor force after marriage or the birth of a child.

Other factors were responsible for the low participation rate of Italian women in wage labor. For example, the few light industries that existed in Milwaukee, such as steam laundries and shoe manufacturing, were located in other areas of the city, beyond the proximity of the Third Ward, where the majority of Italians lived. As in the case of Endicott, Italian women were more likely to engage in wage labor if a workshop was located within walking distance of their homes. Mario Carini, former Third Ward resident and Italian Community Center historian, observes, "Italian women never left the Third Ward. Even if they had to go downtown they would go with their children or send their children."[9]

Italian women in Milwaukee were further limited from participating in wage labor because of labor preferences in hiring practices. This was noted in several Third Ward garment shops that employed German and, later, Irish workers. Germans were often floor ladies and were more likely to hire their own countrywomen before hiring Italian women. Even shoe factories, which typically employed women for gender-specific jobs (as they did at the Endicott Johnson Corporation), were not an option for Italian women in Milwaukee. Most shoe factories were located outside the Third Ward and were also dominated by Germans. "One curious phase of this particular branch of industry," reported a Wisconsin labor study, "are the small factories on the outskirts of Milwaukee, places that are but little more than home shops, with the proprietor's wife acting as bookkeeper or forewoman and the proprietor's relatives and neighbors running the machines."[10]

Because of the economic structure of the city, few light industries located in remote parts of the city, and ethnic preferences in hiring, few Italian women of the immigrant generation in Milwaukee engaged in wage labor. Surveys revealed that Italians and Russian Jews had the smallest proportion of wives working outside the home in Milwaukee.[11] But that is not to say that Italian wives did not earn income. Italian women in Milwaukee turned to other sources for making money. As one report noted, "the proportion of families keeping boarders or lodgers among South Italians is so large as to make the proportion of wives who contribute to the family fund higher than in any other race." In addition to taking in boarders, the study confirmed that "the largest proportion of households engaged in business for profit were found among the Russian Jews and Italians."[12] It is interesting to note the similarity between Italians and Russian Jews in Milwaukee. Both groups of women had the lowest participation rates in wage labor outside the home, yet they had the highest rates of immigrant women who earned income through business endeavors. Italians and Russian Jews responded similarly to the economic structure of the city and the needs of their respective ethnic communities.

An analysis of women's work experiences in Milwaukee reveals that the majority of married Italian women who earned income did so by engaging in business activities. Business activities represent a second occupational option for immigrant women: Italian women met the growing demands and needs of the ethnic enclave. They also reflect the second model of Italian women's work patterns: women who were motivated to earn an income while simultaneously continuing their familial and household responsibilities.

At the turn of the century, the American economy consisted of a considerable number of small businesses. This was particularly evident in cities of large immigrant populations where an ethnic subeconomy evolved, consisting of ethnic-owned enterprises. According to Ewa Morawska, "Ethnic enclaves serve an important purpose during the first phase of immigrants' entry into the U.S. economic system."[13] Shopkeepers met the demands of fellow townspeople for familiar goods and services; women worked in their own kitchens, cooking and cleaning for boarders; and wives and mothers served behind the counter in family-run stores and groceries.

Businessmen who knew consumer tastes and the place to purchase ethnic products dominated the sector of business that provided ethnic foods to immigrant families. According to Donna Gabaccia, wholesale groceries operated by Germans and other Central Europeans dominated food importing from Europe, while "Chinese importers in San Francisco organized a Chinese Chamber of Commerce in the 1880s to keep abreast of customs and tariff regulations affecting their trade."[14] Immigrants, both men and women, who operated smaller businesses displayed the same business acumen as immigrants in the wholesale sector.

Women in family businesses have been a way of life for many immigrant wives, mothers, and young girls. German and East European Jews, as well as Chinese, Greek, Mexican, and other immigrants, often founded small retail businesses catering to ethnic or American consumers. Italians living in Phoenix, Arizona, in 1910, for example, operated restaurants, saloons, grocery stores, and candy shops. Oregon had five thousand Italians in that same year who were proprietors of restaurants, fruit and vegetable markets, and bakeries.[15] Immigrant women worked behind the counters in New York City, where in 1938, almost ten thousand groceries catered exclusively to Italians and an equal number to Jews.[16]

Very little has been written about Italian women's entrepreneurial endeavors and how they served the immigrant community. Kathie Friedman-Kasaba suggests that "most of this work has gone unrecorded except as scattered in short stories, novels, and some memoirs and oral testimonies."[17] When it is acknowledged, immigrant women's participation in a family business is viewed, according to Nancy Foner, as "an extension of a woman's proper role as her husband's helpmate."[18] Defining women's participation in business as "helpmate," however, often obscures their active roles as independent entrepreneurs.

The following examination of businesswomen sheds light on the contributions that immigrant women made in creating and fostering a female business culture in the ethnic community. I also propose new ways of thinking about these occupations and the women who engaged in them. Included in my discussion of businesswomen are Italians who provided services to the ethnic community by taking in boarders, operating retail establishments and food enterprises, and providing skilled services as dressmakers. Gender and domestic values were instrumental in shaping Italian women's working lives in Milwaukee. Nowhere is this clearer than in the case of Italian businesswomen.

Stretching the Limits of Opportunity: Taking in Boarders

We rarely think of the women who kept boarders as businesswomen, entre-preneurs, or innovators. Yet the need for housing posed a serious problem for Italians in Milwaukee who desired to live near their compatriots. Over-crowding in the Third Ward remained a serious problem for years to come as new immigrants took up residence in households willing to provide board-ing services.

Industrious immigrant women around the United States created impor-tant income-generating opportunities by providing boarding services, most often to their compatriots. Keeping boarders, as noted by several historians, was not limited to Italians. Thousands of East European Jews arrived in American cities and provided a steady stream of boarders for women who provided them with meals and a place to sleep.[19] Patricia Preciado Martin writes about Mexican women who ran boarding houses and provided three meals a day for miners who worked in Arizona's copper mines.[20] And in San Francisco's Chinatown, Judy Yung reports that 20 percent of Chinese households had an average of two to three boarders in 1920.[21]

A study conducted by the Immigration Commission in 1911 revealed that boarders and lodgers constituted a larger proportion of the members of Italian households than among any other nationality group in Milwaukee, a result, no doubt, of the preponderance of immigrant males during the early years of Italian settlement. In 1910, for example, 61.1 percent of all Ital-ians in Milwaukee were male,[22] with 40 percent (60 of 149) of Italian house-holds providing services to two and three boarders per household.[23]

Taking in boarders was a business enterprise that fell strictly within a woman's domain. Women offered room and board that included meals and often laundry services in return for cash. Assunta Curri recalled her im-migrant mother's responsibilities for boarders:

> She would have to wash all of their clothes by hand and they worked at the wire factory or at the railroad. Their clothes were filled with grease. Meals were nothing special. They ate what we ate—beans, greens, homemade bread—and my mother would often have to bake four or five loaves of bread a day to feed the family and the boarders. She washed dishes late into the night while my father and the boarders drank homemade wine and played cards.[24]

The numbers of boarders a woman took in could contribute substantially to the family's income. Rose Verrico recalled that, in 1925, a single male paid approximately fifteen dollars a month for room and board. This same male was a wire weaver earning about twenty-four dollars a week in the factory.[25] Therefore, a woman taking in three or four boarders a month earned nearly three-fifths of a factory worker's salary.

Single males and married men with spouses remaining in Italy made up the greatest percentage of boarders. In addition, family members boarded with kin who had established themselves earlier. Boarding provided newly arrived immigrants a supportive environment. Surrounded by compatriots and conversing in their native language while eating familiar foods helped ease immigrants' transition to American life and the loneliness they undoubtedly faced.

Since keeping boarders allowed wives to earn money while remaining at home (thus combining economic, household, and child-rearing tasks), it is often perceived as something other than work. Many scholars regard the services provided to boarders as an extension of women's roles within the home rather than a business endeavor. It was however, a business like any other, where services were provided in return for cash.

Some historians have viewed the Italian practice of keeping boarders as a preferable option to women working outside the home. In her study of Buffalo, Virginia Yans found that Italian women were more likely than any other ethnic group to supplement the family income by taking in boarders. She suggests that Italian women favored this method of earning money rather than working outside the home "unsupervised by relatives or friends."[26] The second model of Italian women's work patterns might better explain this conclusion: those who were motivated to earn an income while simultaneously continuing their familial and household responsibilities. Women who took in boarders were often married and had very young children, allowing them an opportunity to earn income without ever leaving home.

Taking in boarders was, in fact, a sharp break with the Italian past and in many ways reflects Italian women's willingness to adapt to the demands of a new environment. The practice of taking in boarders did not exist in Italy or Sicily, since a household and its house was defined by the nuclear family.[27]

Closer scrutiny of this business venture also suggests that there were risks involved in taking boarders into one's home, risks that were equal to those faced by women working outside the home. With the majority of boarders either single males or men whose wives remained in Italy, prospects for unwanted sexual advances or romantic relationships between boarders and the women who provided these services were heightened. Abraham Cahan raised this issue in a novel about immigrant Jews set on the Lower East Side, wherein an illicit love affair transpires between Dora and her boarder, David Levinsky.[28]

Sources reveal that clandestine affairs were not merely fiction but often occurred in boarding households. Rose Carini, a Sicilian immigrant to Milwaukee, recalled that "young male boarders often fell in love with the daughters of the family they were boarding with." In one instance, she claims, "the father of the household told the boarder he had to move out before he could consider 'appropriately' courting his daughter."[29] In another instance, Maria, who lived in rented rooms with her immigrant parents, recalls that her father moved the family into their own home because he feared that his wife and daughter would be vulnerable to sexual advances by males boarding in the same household.[30] In 1918, sixteen-year-old Antonia B. was forced into marriage by her father after a romantic tryst with a boarder ended in pregnancy.[31] And in 1911, a sexual encounter ended in tragedy when an Italian husband in Wisconsin returned from work to find his wife in bed with the boarder and killed them both.[32] Taking in boarders, a business that kept Italian women at home, did not necessarily safeguard them from contact with the opposite sex.

The practice of providing services to boarders had its risks, but it provided women with an opportunity to earn money at a stage during their life cycle when they were caring for young children. According to census data for Milwaukee, in 1905, for example, of 132 Italian households with wives present, 56 (42 percent) took in boarders. Of these 56 households, 38 of them (68 percent) took in boarders who were unrelated to the family, while 18 households (32 percent) provided boarding to family members. For the most part, wives who provided boarding services had young children at home (52 percent), but several older women who were widows, as well as young married women with no children, also engaged in this line of work.

Young married women without children who provided boarding services were immigrants who had been in the United States only a short time. This is supported in a 1911 report of immigrants in Milwaukee, indicating that 74 percent of households providing boarding services were Italians who had been in the United States five years or less. It appears that the longer that Italians resided in the United States, the less inclined they were to take in boarders. For Italians who had been in Milwaukee five to nine years, the percentage of households keeping boarders drops to 40.8 percent, while among those Italians who had been living in Milwaukee ten years and over, only 19 percent were keeping boarders.[33] Indeed, the number of households with boarders steadily declined, indicating a decrease in single male transients and the growing stability of the Italian family.

Thus, for young married Italian women who had recently arrived in Milwaukee, keeping boarders was one of the easiest and quickest ways to earn income. In addition, these women were engaged in a line of business that was favorable to the establishment and maintenance of the immigrant community.

Minding the Store

As noted above, the Immigration Commission's report of 1911 stated that the largest proportion of households engaged in business for profit was found among the Russian Jews and Italians. Italian women played a unique role in the development of businesses in the Third Ward. Immigrant women, whose presence as business proprietors and retail merchants in Milwaukee was recorded in city directories and the state census as early as 1900, were actively engaged in every field of Italian business enterprise during the lengthy period of first-generation settlement, from 1900 to the 1930s.

Gender and domestic values were instrumental in shaping Italian women's job opportunities in Milwaukee. Nowhere is this clearer than in the case of Italian businesswomen. Immigrants who had been small-business proprietors in Italy founded some of Milwaukee's most profitable produce companies, and a number of them included the wife and mother as business partner.

Perhaps the most notable example was Mary Pastorino, whose husband, Frank, was one of the earliest commission merchants in the Third Ward. After emigrating from Italy, Frank and Mary relocated in 1891 from Chicago to Milwaukee, where they bought a wholesale produce business located on Commission Row. Frank and his partner, Louis Schiappacasse, became successful wholesale dealers in domestic and foreign fruits, vegetables, and nuts.[34] Mary frequently accompanied her husband to Central America and advised him on purchasing fruits, dates, nuts, and other produce, and she also operated a confectionery shop, the Flora Bon. In 1910, Frank died and left controlling interest of the business to his wife. Sons Harry and Frank worked with their mother in the business until Mary sold her shares to Schiappacasse a few years later, giving him controlling interest of the business. Mary Pastorino had not left the world of business however; several years later she opened a tearoom, where she employed several of her daughters.[35]

There were other Italian women whose contributions to a business enterprise have never been appreciated fully because they too worked alongside their husbands in family-owned businesses. Mrs. Caravalla worked behind the counter in her husband's drugstore, and, together, Maria and Sebastiano operated Gagliano's Flower Shop. Rose Tocco assisted her husband in his bakery, waiting on customers and occasionally preparing fancy cookies for special occasions, while Vincenza Minnoia made candy and ice cream alongside her husband in their confectionery shop.[36]

The Catalanos were very successful fruit and produce wholesalers who in 1911 shifted the center of their business to home, most likely because it was more profitable than renting a wholesale house. Mrs. Catalano's role in the business was instrumental; she handled the banking and kept the books.[37]

Italian-born women who themselves launched various business establishments in Milwaukee exhibited the range of marital patterns. While a few were single women or widows who had inherited a husband's business, most were married women who operated their business independently of their husband's employment or enterprise. Jennie Ferraro, who was twenty-five at the time of the 1920 census, was married to a wagon driver and owned and operated her own bakery. Mary La Barbara worked in her husband's butcher shop on Jefferson Street, where former Third Ward residents recall her "hauling slabs of meat over her shoulder." Anna DiMaggio worked as a seamstress while her husband was alive but took over his butcher shop after his death. Anna's eldest son was employed as a manager of the shop, and her youngest son was a meat cutter, but Anna and her daughter assisted in grinding the sausage and other meats. Fanny Alberti took over her father's butcher shop when he passed away. Anna DiMaggio and Fanny Alberti were typical of female proprietors who surfaced in typically "unfeminine" pursuits. These were often widows who assumed the places of departed husbands or daughters who assumed the place of a departed parent when there was no son to take over the family business.

Italian women were also engaged in other "unfeminine" pursuits, such as the manufacture of moonshine. In interviews with former Third Ward residents, they revealed that during prohibition soft drink establishments were used to conceal the manufacture and sale of liquor. Bellina Chiaverotti advertised as a soft drink provider, but the bottles she sold were filled with moonshine. Mrs. Buscaglia ran a fruit stand but tucked away home brew for sale. Lucretia Sanfellippo and her daughter, Maria, operated the Alamo, where they made and sold soda, along with beer and wine. Interviews with Milwaukee Italians reveal that many Italian wives made the alcohol, and their husbands sold it. In fact, some women, such as Emilia Colla, were bootleggers in their own right.[38] "Blackie" Brocca recalls that "my mom and dad made moonshine together," supplementing the family economy nicely.[39] According to the Milwaukee City Directories, Lillian Agostino, Josephine Bareta, Vincenza Paolo, and Victoria Rompola were several other Italian women who owned and operated "soft drink" establishments during the years of prohibition. Milwaukee women were not the only Italian women involved in bootlegging during the dry years in Wisconsin. In nearby Madison, the capital of the state, Jennie Justo (Vincenza DiGilormo), was dubbed by government investigators in the Wickersham Commission Report on Prohibition the "Queen of Bootleggers." Following her father's murder as part of a mob vendetta, Jennie operated a speakeasy from her home in order to support her five younger siblings.[40]

Rose Maniaci and Conchetta Pistoria operated dry-goods stores, and one of the few northern Italians to live in the Third Ward, Mrs. Rachiti, owned and operated a small cigar-manufacturing enterprise located within her home. She employed several Sicilian women, whose occupations were listed in the city directory as cigar makers, an occupation that, in Milwaukee, as in other American cities, employed large numbers of women.[41]

Most of these businesses were conducted primarily at home, while the family lived above or behind the establishment. However, some women also ran businesses that were not home-based, though still located within the ethnic community. Several of them were the proprietors of confectionery shops in the Third Ward. In 1900, following her husband's murder by the Black Hand, Theresa Balbi opened a fruit stand and after several years became a confectioner, employing her daughter, Lillie, as a clerk. Jeanette Corti, a single woman who immigrated from Italy to Milwaukee in 1905, became the proprietor of a confectionery store, where she made candy and ice cream. As noted earlier, Mary Pastorino, the wife of a leading produce merchant, started a small confectionery shop called the Flora Bon, where she put her nine children to work dipping chocolates.

The Milwaukee City Directories documents twenty-nine Italian saloons in the Third Ward in 1915. These were owned and operated mainly by men. Yet female entrepreneurs emerged even in this predominantly male enterprise; these included Antonia Natoli, Julia Faganelli, Anna Loffredo, and others.

Italian women participated in the family and community economy through food enterprises, working as proprietors and cooks in their own restaurants.

Women who operated neighborhood restaurants assumed multiple chores, combining cooking with serving patrons and dishwashing. Neighborhood restaurants occupied a small space, with a few tables and chairs, similar to Italian *trattorias*. Typically, there were no menus, and women served whatever they happened to cook that day or what was fresh, according to the season. Pasta with a simple tomato sauce was a staple of all neighborhood restaurants. Women often prepared greens, such as escarole sautéd in garlic and olive oil and *minestra* or *pasta fagioli* with homemade bread.

Eventually, several restaurants grew larger and more commercial, catering not only to the ethnic enclave but the larger Milwaukee community as well. Among the women whose eating establishments evolved into prosperous restaurants were Mary Romano, proprietor of Madam Romano's Restaurant; Vincenza Zizzo, owner of the Venice Club; Agatha Corradero, who operated a pizzeria and restaurant; and Mamie Gigliotta, owner and cook at Mimi's Grotto. Rose Maniaci, whose restaurant, the Canadian Club, was among the best known in Milwaukee, provided free meals to Marquette University students for over thirty-five years.[42]

Italian restaurants were essential to the development of the ethnic community. Through their cooking, Italian women sustained food traditions that had originated in their local *paese* and provided "a structure upon which a coherent group identity could be built and maintained" in America. Italians used the role of food "as a visceral reminder of the past," according to Tracy Poe, "and a tangible marker of the future in which they hoped to participate." For Italians, food "offered a symbol of home and community around which people from different regions, classes, and political opinions could naturally congregate."[43] Italian women, while preserving regional and ethnic food traditions, were instrumental in creating an important part of communal life and ethnic identity.

Italian Grocers: Women behind the Counter

Italian women played a unique role in the development and maintenance of food traditions and businesses in their neighborhoods. Food businesses, especially grocery stores, were particularly important for linking home and workplace and for creating communities of grocers and their clientele. Family-owned grocery stores linked home and workplace, not only for the reason that businesses were located within the family home, but because immigrant mothers utilized the labor of their children. Young boys often helped their mothers stock shelves, while young women kept watch over the store while their mothers slipped back to the kitchen to prepare an evening meal.

Of the forty-five grocery establishments owned by Milwaukee's Italians in 1915, thirty-eight of them were located in the Third Ward. Mary Maglio, a Sicilian and the first Italian-born female grocer in Milwaukee, had opened one of them on Detroit Street in 1905. Many other Italian women followed suit, becoming proprietors of home-based grocery stores. Merely a year later, Angela Azzarello, Isabella D'Amore, Mary D'Amore, and Bella Rodino were all listed as grocery-store owners. This Milwaukee pattern of female Italian-owned businesses became more common in the 1920s and early 1930s, as these small concerns proliferated in immigrant neighborhoods across the country. John Bodnar explains that these enterprises "were easier to start in an era when monopoly capital had not yet replaced the pattern of commercial capitalism."[44] With very little capital investment and virtually no overhead, immigrant families could, in their own homes, start business establishments serving the immigrant community.

According to Kathleen Conzen, who conducted a study of Irish and Germans in Milwaukee, by the 1860s a clear business pattern had emerged, with immigrants concentrated in local retail establishments and the native-born dominant in regional commerce and wholesaling. More specifically, the grocery business was the type of merchandising that most attracted the Irish and Germans.[45] By the early 1900s, Italians were emerging as business leaders in local retail as well.

Compared to other regions in the country, proportionately Milwaukee had a large number of businesses owned by Italian women. Historian Luciano Iorizzo notes that nationwide in the late nineteenth century only 7 percent of all merchants were Italian American women, whereas, among the nearly 130 Italian-owned grocery stores operating in the Third Ward between 1900 and 1920, 40 (32.5 percent) were owned and operated by women.[46] All forty of these women had been born in Italy, the majority of them in Sicily.[47] They included women like Mary Serio, who migrated to Milwaukee in 1889; the wife of a fruit dealer, she ran a grocery store while she raised her nine children. Similarly, Francesca Maglio, the mother of seven children, came to Milwaukee in 1902 and operated a grocery store.[48]

Italian women who owned grocery stores were either married or recently widowed. The majority of the female proprietors of grocery stores (68 percent) were married to men gainfully employed. Francesca Maglio's husband was a laborer, for example, and Theresa Sottili's husband, a carpenter. Women who operated grocery stores often were married to men who were also in business. Sarah Caravella's and Theresa Corso's husbands, for instance, owned saloons, while Mary Serio and Angie Spicuzza were married to fruit dealers.[49]

Of the 40 women, at least 8 women (20 percent) were widows and took over the grocery business after their husbands died. They included Mary Tornabene, whose husband, Beniamino, had been a grocer from 1904 through 1910. In 1911, she became a widow and the proprietor of the business. An immigrant in Milwaukee since 1891, Rosa D'Amore took over Agostino's store when he died in 1906, and for years thereafter she was able to support herself and her three children.[50] Another enterprising widow was Catherine D'Aquisto, born in Porticello, Sicily, in 1884. As a young girl she was sent to Palermo to help care for the children of a wealthy family. During her free time, she watched the cook prepare meals and thus began a lifelong love affair with food. In 1900, Catherine immigrated alone to America to live and work with her sister, who had a bakery in New York City. Several years later she joined another sister living in Milwaukee, where she met and married her husband, Joseph Dentice, a recently arrived Sicilian from Sant'Elia and a fruit peddler in the Third Ward. While her children were young, Catherine earned extra income by cooking and baking in her home for weddings and baptisms. No longer a fruit peddler but a city employee, Joseph was still unable to provide a sufficient income for his family, so Catherine decided to start her own grocery store. Shelves loaded with macaroni, tomatoes, oranges, and bananas filled the front room of the family home. Catherine also baked bread every morning and sold it to her customers for a nickel a loaf. While remaining at home and raising her four children, Catherine later turned her talents into yet more income by cooking and baking for the immigrant neighborhood and operating a grocery store specializing in Italian food products.[51]

Gender, Domestic Values, and Home-based Business

Two case studies of Sicilian-born women who operated grocery stores in the Third Ward reveal how immigrant women's working lives in business, too, were shaped by domestic values and the life cycle. Both women operated small grocery stores at home. Front rooms were emptied of furniture, and shelving went up where pictures and shrines to the Virgin Mary had once hung. The shelves were stocked with olive oil, imported pasta, olives, tomatoes, homemade bread, and fresh fruits. These enterprising women created the opportunity to run a business while taking care of homes and raising children. Children, however, were not exempt from the responsibilities of the home-based business. In fact, businesswomen frequently encouraged, indeed expected, their children to share the responsibilities of running the store.

Maria Latona exhibits a pattern that scholars have identified as an important component of the Italian family-run business: "Family members were expected to contribute their labor to the family business, thereby maximizing operating hours and minimizing operating costs."[52] Maria and Salvatore Latona migrated with their four children to Milwaukee in 1909 from Bagheria, Sicily. Salvatore found work, as did many other Italian men, at the Department of Public Works, while Maria contributed a little extra to the family economy by taking in boarders. Still, the couple could not comfortably support their family, which soon grew to eight. In response, Salvatore and Maria also became small-business owners. In 1914, Salvatore opened a tavern, while also maintaining his city job, and Maria, who continued to accept boarders, started a grocery store that she operated from six in the morning until eight at night.

Maria's work life also was closely intertwined with that of her two daughters, Domenica and Vincenza. The eldest daughter, Domenica, was thirteen when she arrived in Milwaukee with her parents; a year later she married and, at age fifteen, gave birth to her first child. She and her husband and their growing family lived upstairs over her parents' grocery store and tavern. In order to help Domenica and her husband provide for their children, Maria turned the grocery store over to her daughter, who expanded the store's inventory with jewelry and children's clothing. In 1932, Domenica's husband died, leaving her a widow with nine children to support. When the grocery store could not sustain her large family, Domenica took a full-time job at Cohn Brothers sewing men's garments, and her mother returned to the grocery store, giving most of the profits over to her daughter. This arrangement allowed Maria to care for her nine grandchildren while her daughter worked in the factory. According to Maria's daughters, "When the children returned home from school in the afternoon, the older ones were expected to help their grandmother in the grocery store by stocking shelves and relieving *nonna* while she prepared the evening meal and tended to the younger children."[53]

Several years later, Maria's youngest daughter, Vincenza, was married, but by this time, Maria and Salvatore were no longer running the tavern or grocery store. Their home, the grocery store, and the tavern had been destroyed when the Black Hand planted a bomb in retribution for Salvatore's refusal to comply with an extortion demand.[54] Maria, Salvatore, Domenica, and her nine children were forced to move in with Vincenza and her husband. One year later, Vincenza's husband died of a heart attack, leaving the young widow with six small children to support. "With my sister's help," Vincenza recalled, "I was hired at Cohn Brothers. My mother continued caring for Domenica's youngest children, but now she had six more grandchildren to tend, the youngest only a year old."[55]

A second case similarly illustrates the influence of gender and family values in Italian immigrant households. In the late 1880s, Conchetta and Joseph Burgerino left their small village near Palermo for Milwaukee's Third Ward and opened a grocery store on Detroit Street. The 1920 census lists Joseph as the store's proprietor, but it was Conchetta who operated the business while raising six children. Unable to read or write, Conchetta nevertheless could keep charge accounts by creating symbols for her customers and marking "X" next to the symbol each time they paid on their accounts. When Conchetta got too old for the business, her eldest daughter, Anna Torretta, also born in Sicily, took over the business and repeated her mother's work patterns, operating the store while raising her children. Anna walked several blocks to Commission Row every morning to select fresh produce to sell, and in the summer she made Italian ice and sold it on the street in front of her store. Having operated one business successfully, Anna, whose husband was always seasonally employed, opened another grocery on the south side of Milwaukee, where, according to her daughter, "she also did a great business making homemade wine."[56] Anna took her eldest daughter, Josephine (later, Rampolla), into the grocery business and proceeded to open two more stores in other locations. Torretta and Rampolla were still listed as grocers in the 1930 city directory. Anna also expanded one of the grocery stores to include a butcher shop and did almost all the butchering herself. A tavern was eventually opened adjacent to the grocery store, run by Anna's son-in-law, while daughter Josephine also helped out by serving up fish fries on Friday night, chicken on Saturday, and potato pancakes on Wednesday.

Anna had taken her daughter out of school at sixteen to start her in the family business. Josephine proudly recalls her busy mother "running the grocery, making homemade wine, and raising four children." For her part, Josephine continued working for her mother until her own marriage, and, later, when her youngest child was two-and-a-half years old, she started her own business, a very successful catering operation that she conducted for twenty-two years. She credits her business career, and that of her siblings, to her mother; as she put it, "[We] all had this business background from my mom."[57] In the Burgerino family, the spirit of entrepreneurship passed from mother to daughter.

For Italian-born women, the motives for starting a business were similar to the entrepreneurial motives of Italian men. Ethnic economic enclaves often emerged as a result of discriminatory policies or of job discrimination in majority labor markets.[58] Immigrant entrepreneurs used language and cultural barriers and ethnic affinities to gain privileged access to markets.[59]

Limited by education and language, they recognized the needs of the immigrant community and viewed business ownership as a means of achieving economic and familial goals within the boundaries of their ethnic neighborhoods. Gender, however, helped shape these women's decisions. Operating a business in their home allowed them to combine economic activities with domestic responsibilities. Moreover, small-business operations that evolved within the homes of immigrant businesswomen were a means of upward mobility for themselves as well as for their children. Restaurants and grocery stores worked as intersections of Italian ethnic identity and American commercialism and, in both enterprises, Italian women played a major role.

Dressmakers

A skill that most Italian women brought with them from Italy was sewing. Many young women were trained in lacework and embroidery, while others became seamstresses and dressmakers.[60]

In Milwaukee the Italian dressmakers' shops resembled those of other dressmakers at the turn of the century, women who worked out of their homes, allowing them to remain on the site of family responsibilities. Maria Stella, Anna Dionizi, Rose Antonucci, Jennie Orlando, and Anna Turano were among Italian women who, during the first two decades of the twentieth century, established their trade as dressmakers in the Third Ward. Working out of their homes or in small neighborhood workshops, dressmakers, like grocers, catered to the needs of the ethnic community.

Conducting business considered within women's sphere, dressmakers employed other women, writes Wendy Gamber, "while men were totally excluded from their domain."[61] They were part of a larger craft tradition in America that provided a lucrative trade for immigrants as well as for native-born Americans.

Perhaps the best documentation of a historical dressmaking business in the United States is a recent study of the Tirocchi sisters' workshop in Providence, Rhode Island. Trained in Italy in custom dressmaking, Anna and Laura Tirocchi transplanted their craft to the United States and established a thriving dressmaking business, catering to the wealthy elite of Providence.

Between 1915 and 1931, the Tirocchi sisters employed an average of twelve to sixteen girls in their workshop, the majority of whom were daughters of Italian immigrants.[62]

Other immigrant women who were skilled dressmakers in their native land transplanted their skills to America and used them as a means of upward mobility. Rose Caricato and her daughter, Giulia, for example, were expert dressmakers and carried on an extremely successful business at home, catering to Italians and other residents of their upstate New York community. They became so successful that they were engaged to design and sew wedding apparel for many affluent families.[63] Eventually, Giulia opened a women's clothing store, while her mother continued working as a seamstress in her daughter's dress shop.

A more recent immigrant to Wisconsin, Maria Fabiano, learned to sew as a ten-year-old girl in Italy. Fabiano perfected her skills at a school in Cosenza, where she learned how to create patterns and make dresses for custom order. After settling in Wisconsin in 1962, she opened her own dressmaking shop, where she continues to design clothing for participants in the Miss Wisconsin pageant and formal wear for the Presidential Inaugural Ball.[64]

While Italian dressmakers in Milwaukee did not achieve the economic and social status of businesswomen such as the Tirocchis, they managed, nonetheless, to support themselves, many of them even training their daughters in their craft. Several dressmakers in the Third Ward, such as Francesca Romano and Jennie Gallo, trained and employed their daughters in their businesses with them.

Within a decade of settlement in Milwaukee's Third Ward, Italians had created the most homogeneous ethnic community in the city. The needs of the immigrant community for goods and services provided a ready-made market for shopkeepers who established themselves in the ethnic enclave. The overlap of home and workplace meant that women and children often worked together, and more important, women with children could conduct business without ever leaving home.

Work outside the Home

Work patterns reveal that Italian women who worked outside the home in Milwaukee were either single or newly married with no children. Married women who had children and no relatives or neighbors to care for the children simply had to find other means of earning an income. The majority of

Italian women who worked in factories were young and single and often worked for several years, but either quit when they were married or after the birth of a child. There were very few light industries in the Third Ward, and the prevalent working conditions discouraged Italian wives from pursuing employment.

Young Italian-born girls, along with the daughters of immigrants, often quit school at an early age to contribute to the family economy, a pattern consistent with immigrant working patterns in Endicott and other cities. As Bodnar observes, "The percentage of wage earners among foreign-born adult females over the age of sixteen was one-third higher than the percentage for all white women, but this could be attributed to the heavier reliance of the immigrant family on the earnings of their unmarried daughters."[65] Catherine Balistreri was typical of immigrant daughters who labored for the good of the family: she attended school until the eighth grade but then had to quit in order to help support her widowed mother. She worked at Phoenix Hosiery and handed her weekly pay envelope to her mother, "who gave me spending money for an occasional soda or ice cream."[66] A 1911 study reported that, among young girls working in light industry in Milwaukee, "only 78 of the 1,189 girls are boarding away from home" and that "875 of those living with parents or close relatives contribute their entire earnings to the family income, while 202 pay board at home."[67]

Immigrant daughters in Milwaukee, similar to those in Endicott, had a strong understanding of their families' needs, but longed to use some of their earnings on consumer items and American pastimes. Intergenerational conflict often exploded in immigrant families over the familial expectations of daughters' wages, as Vicki Ruiz found in her study of Mexican women in California. An immigrant woman might rationalize her wage-earning role as an extension of her family responsibilities, but her U.S.-born daughter might visualize her own income as an avenue to independence.[68]

Those Italian women employed outside the home in Milwaukee worked in establishments within walking distance of their homes, as they did in Endicott. Many girls were employed as packers and dippers at the American Candy Company on Buffalo Street, the Imperial Candy Company on East Water, and the Princess Confectionery Company on Jefferson Street, all located in the Third Ward. Candy companies located in the Third Ward offered employment opportunities that were clearly "feminine." However, a closer examination of the conditions of work in these establishments reveals why it was an occupation better suited for young single women rather than married women, especially those with children.

A 1911 study conducted by the Milwaukee Bureau of Economy and Effi-ciency, examined 1,189 working girls under twenty-one years of age who were employed in candy, glove, and paper box factories and clothing establish-ments. The study reported that "the physical conditions in the factories are mainly satisfactory . . . they being clean, light, fairly well ventilated and the machinery properly safeguarded." The exceptions were two candy factories and one clothing establishment. Italian girls labored in poor conditions in candy factories, working from fifty-four to sixty hours per week. During the rush season, the workweek was extended to "80, 84 or even 90 hours per week."[69] One labor investigation reported that "wages were proverbially poor and no industry requires more over-time than do the candy factories. For almost two months before Christmas, the factories are run until 8 and 9 and even 10 o'clock at night to keep up the orders that came in from all over the country."[70] The demands of working in Milwaukee's candy factories were nearly impossible for wives and mothers. In Endicott, by contrast, Italian women employed in the shoe factories worked a forty-hour week with flex-ible hours that were designed to accommodate working mothers.

Other examples of Italian women's work experiences in Milwaukee's fac-tories reflect the impact of marriage and family on labor-force participation. Rose Carini, who immigrated to Milwaukee with her parents at the age of two, attended schools in the Third Ward but "when I turned fourteen," she stated, "I was allowed to work at Phoenix Hosiery during summer vacations, where I earned fifteen cents an hour."[71] Rose continued working at Phoenix Hosiery until her marriage and the birth of her children.

At fifteen, having received ship fare from her sister, Emma Bellucci set off alone for Milwaukee. Shortly after her arrival, with the help of other im-migrant women, she was hired at David Adler and Sons; she continued there after her marriage but quit following the birth of her first child. After giving birth to two more children, Emma began taking in homework sewing but-tonholes on clothing provided by Adler's garment factory.[72]

Vincenza Bartolone and Conchetta Crivello were sisters who were both widowed in their thirties; they were able to take jobs at Cohn Brothers because they had a mother who willingly cared for their fifteen children while they labored in the garment factory.[73] The work profile of Balistreri and other women indicate how the family economy shaped immigrant lives.

Immigrant women and their daughters had more opportunities to work outside the home beginning in the 1920s, with the establishment of several garment factories, such as David Adler and Sons, Cohn Brothers, Moritz and Winter, and Phoenix Hosiery. Unfortunately, no employment records exist for these establishments, so it is impossible to know the exact numbers of the Italian women employed there. However, census data for Milwaukee reveal that by the late 1920s and 1930s, second-generation Italian women were beginning to enter garment factories as they became established in areas close to and within the Third Ward.

Because of the relatively few clothing factories in Milwaukee, there was little opportunity for immigrant women to do homework. Homework represents the first type of work described earlier. Prompted by a segmented labor market and the growing demand for female workers, it was a female industry that could be carried out at home. Yet, the women who engaged in homework fit the second model, representing Italian women who were motivated to earn an income while simultaneously continuing their familial and household responsibilities.

A few garment factories located in the Third Ward and some downtown department stores generated work that could be finished at home. Few reliable statistics exist for assessing the number of actual homeworkers in Milwaukee, but a 1915 survey reported that only "a very limited" number of women "take outside work into the home, generally sewing and hand embroidering for factories, either because the work is scarce, or poorly remunerated."[74] The most highly paid was a woman who did beautiful hand embroidery and received five dollars per week, while the most poorly paid was a mother with two daughters, who, for mending sacks at two cents each, could not make more than three dollars per week.[75]

Women who had learned fine sewing in Italy commanded the best wages in Milwaukee, including Rose Carini's mother, who had learned to embroider while at a convent school in Sicily. A sample of her work prompted Gimbel's and T. A. Chapman's department stores to hire her to do fine embroidery on shirts, blouses, dresses, and babies' clothing. Rose picked up the materials and brought them home, where her mother worked on them in between cooking meals and caring for the children.[76] American-born children were instrumental in acting as go-betweens for their immigrant mothers' wage-earning opportunities. American-born children of immigrant parents often assumed the role of translator for parents who could not speak English. It was common practice for merchant and factory representatives from T. A. Chapman's and Gimbel's department stores, as well as David Adler and Sons and Cohen Brothers garment factories, to contact Third Ward schoolchildren about work opportunities for their mothers. Children were sent home to enlist their mothers in homework. Immigrant women took advantage of these opportunities to earn money at home and did everything from fancy stitching and copying patterns for department stores to trimming and sewing hems and linings in coats for clothing factories. Children were also instrumental as runners for the stores and factories that delegated finishing work to immigrant women. Runners, according to Mario Carini, "were young children who picked up the garments and distributed them to their mothers and other homeworkers and then returned them to the manufacturer when they were finished."[77]

Many women who had worked at home while their children were young later abandoned homework for factory labor, as did Giovanna Chirafisi; when her children were older, she entered the men's clothing factory that earlier had supplied her with piecework. George LaPiana maintains that "if there was more work and it was better paid, a larger number of Italian women would devote more hours per day to sewing and embroidering, and to assisting the family, especially when the husband is out of work."[78] In Milwaukee homework remained a limited opportunity for immigrant women who wanted to earn money while remaining at home. By contrast, thousands of immigrant women engaged in industrial homework in cities dominated by the garment trade. In New York City, for example, Italian women monopolized homework.[79] Cynthia Daniels indicates that as many as 250,000 immigrant women may have been employed as homeworkers in New York City in 1911, most of whom were between the ages of twenty-five and forty-five, married, and with young children to care for.[80] The U.S. Department of Labor, however, reported that homeworkers were paid less than living wages and worked excessively long hours. In San Antonio, married Mexican American women who were homebound because of childcare responsibilities engaged in garment work, sewing pieces cut in New York City and sent for finishing in Texas. Julia Kirk Blackwelder's study of Mexican American women in Depression-era San Antonio describes the exploitation that homeworkers felt in their jobs. For most Hispanic women, homework was critical to family survival; they worked more than eight hours a day at least six days a week and complained of exhaustion, muscle cramps, and eyestrain.[81]

The supply of labor available to perform industrial homework was abundant. But not all cities had industries to generate an abundance of homework for willing workers, as was the case in Milwaukee. Despite the low wages, homework provided women with a convenient way to earn additional income while remaining at home with their children and continuing traditional domestic responsibilities.

Gender and domestic values helped shape immigrant women's work experiences in the early twentieth century. In Milwaukee the opportunities for women working outside the home were limited because the city's economic base was primarily heavy industry. Married women were further limited because they were confined to the home with small children. Yet, they found productive ways to earn income and remained indispensable partners to their husbands in America.

Italian women's economic adjustment to life in Milwaukee reveals the interplay between Old World lives and New World realities. A large number of businesswomen in Milwaukee came from families who had operated small-business establishments in Italy. This was particularly evident among Sicilians.[82] Similarly, women who established themselves as dressmakers in Milwaukee had been trained as *sarte* in Italy. Their Italian training provided them with skills that were easily transplanted to the United States and one of the ways that women could earn money while remaining at home. Other women adapted to the needs of the immigrant enclave in America by providing boarding and lodging services to their compatriots and by engaging in business ventures as grocers, restaurateurs, saloonkeepers, dressmakers, and purveyors of dry goods.

In all of these activities, gender and domestic values were instrumental in shaping Italian women's working lives. Operating a business at home allowed Italian women to combine economic activities with domestic responsibilities and, at the same time, provided important services to the immigrant community. Their business enterprises helped establish an economic base in the ethnic enclave, while preserving cultural traditions important to sustaining an Italian way of life.

4

Female Professionals in the Immigrant Community: Italian-trained Midwives

ON 21 DECEMBER 1909, Rosa Sperandandio applied for a state license from the Board of Medical Examiners to practice midwifery in the State of Wisconsin. Rosa had studied at the Royal University of Palermo, in Sicily, for two years and received her midwifery diploma on 3 July 1900. The application described Rosa as a woman of "good character, neat, scrupulous and honest."[1] Rosa Sperandandio was typical of Italian-born women practicing midwifery in Milwaukee in the early decades of the twentieth century. She was an immigrant; she was young; and she was educated and professionally trained.

If the example of Milwaukee's businesswomen suggests the need for significant revision of conventional portraits of Italian immigrant workingwomen, the case of Italian midwives offers an especially stark contrast to these familiar images. This select group of professionally trained and educated women brought a professional ethos to their working lives, one that often competed with and, in some cases, overrode obligations of marriage or family.

Italian midwives made up a small number of workingwomen in Milwaukee. However, their unique occupational status, their importance to the cultural milieu of the ethnic community, and their attitudes toward work make them worthy of close analysis.

While different because of educational background and work patterns, businesswomen and midwives were similar in that, as first-generation immigrants, they provided important services to the Italian community. Therefore, midwives are also representative of the second type of work engaged in by Italian women, which served the growing demand and needs of the ethnic enclave.

The greatest numbers of practicing immigrant midwives at the turn of the century were found in cities with large foreign populations. The size of the Italian settlement determined the extent of the need for immigrant midwives. In Manhattan, during 1905, for example, there were between nine hundred and one thousand foreign-born practicing midwives, 25 percent of whom were Italian.[2]

Milwaukee also experienced an influx of foreign-born midwives in the late nineteenth century, due in large part to the substantial numbers of European immigrants. As a *Milwaukee Sentinel* article pointed out in 1889, "No city in the country has as many practicing midwives as Milwaukee; it is said, at least in proportion to population. There are only a comparatively few more physicians than midwives, there being 171 of the former and 115 of the latter."[3]

Only one Italian midwife was recorded in Milwaukee in the late nineteenth century, reflecting the rather insignificant size of the Italian community at that time. However, after 1900, as the Italian community grew, so too, did the number of Italian midwives.

The number of practicing midwives reflected the needs of a community. Even small Italian settlements, like Cortland, in upstate New York, with an Italian-born population of only 608, had one Italian midwife.[4] There were no midwives in Endicott, however, a reflection, in part, of the policies of a community dominated by the Endicott Johnson Corporation and its program of corporate welfare. The majority of Italians in Endicott were employed by Endicott Johnson, which provided both women workers and the wives of workers with full maternity benefits, thus, in effect, minimizing the demand for immigrant midwives.

Milwaukee makes an interesting site for the study of midwives for several reasons. All of the Italian-born midwives who practiced in Milwaukee were professionally trained and certified (unlike other cities, where there were as likely to be many lay practitioners). In addition, Milwaukee boasted two midwifery schools: the Milwaukee School of Midwifery, founded in 1879 by a German-born midwife, and the Wisconsin College of Midwifery, established in 1885 by a German immigrant trained in the United States.[5] Thus, immigrant women who had not been formally trained in Europe had the opportunity for midwifery training in Milwaukee. Furthermore, Wisconsin regulated the practice of midwifery by requiring training, testing, and registration of all practicing midwives.

Beginning in the 1870s and culminating with the 1909 Midwife Registration Act, physicians helped determine which midwives could deliver babies and the conditions under which they could work. Consequently, application and licensing records with information on midwives' training, education, and previous confinement cases, along with other pertinent information, are available for Wisconsin.[6]

In this chapter I investigate the working lives of Italian midwives, a small group of transplanted, trained women who saw themselves as professionals. In contemporary terms, Italian midwives in Wisconsin at the turn of the century were career women for whom work and professional development often competed with marital obligations and family needs.

Similar to female restaurant and grocery-store owners, who played an important role in preserving ethnic identity through food, midwives were instrumental in transferring Old World rituals and practices of childbirth to New World settlements. Practicing in the same ethnic neighborhoods as those women working as dressmakers, saloonkeepers, and retail merchants, midwives went house-to-house delivering the babies of immigrant women who preferred midwife-assisted deliveries by Italian-speaking midwives.

In 1900, the proportion of births attended by midwives in the United States was estimated at 50 percent.[7] Considerable variations occurred in the proportion of births attended by midwives in the early twentieth century, with greater numbers of midwife-assisted births occurring in regions with large immigrant and African American populations. Midwifery was a practice that remained culturally relevant for immigrant women, as it did for southern African American women. In 1913, for example, midwives attended 50 percent of the births in Chicago, 39 percent in New York City, 75 percent in St. Louis, 25 percent in San Francisco, and 70 percent in New Orleans. In Taos County, New Mexico, midwives attended 69 percent of Spanish-surname births from 1933 to 1937.[8]

Some midwives became part of local folklore, as did Magerou, a Greek midwife, who delivered the babies of Greek, Austrian, Italian, and Slavic women whose husbands were miners in the Midvale-Bingham-Magna coal area of Utah during the first decade of the twentieth century.[9] In the Southwest, Jesusita Aragon practiced the traditional Hispanic methods of midwifery learned from her grandmother and subsequently delivered over twelve thousand babies in an isolated, mountainous area of New Mexico.[10] Onnie Lee Logan is remembered as the last "granny midwife" in one of the poorest black counties of Alabama.[11]

Judy Litoff, a scholar of midwifery practices in the United States, explains that at the turn of the twentieth century, immigrant women, especially those newly arrived from southern and eastern Europe, showed a marked preference for midwives. Studies show that Italian women, in particular, preferred midwife-assisted deliveries. This practice is supported by data from major cities of Italian settlement. In Chicago, a 1908 analysis of over one thousand registered births showed that midwives had attended 25 percent of Russian, 68 percent of German, and 86 percent of Italian births.[12] In her study of the New York Midwifery Dispensary (1890–1920), Nancy Schrom Dye found that Italian women used the dispensary's doctors less frequently than did any other immigrant group on the Lower East Side because of their preference for midwives. Of the 10,233 patients who registered between January 1890 and April 1896, only 22 were Italian women, as compared to 6,885 Russian Jewish women.[13] As late as 1924, over three-fourths of Italian-born women on New York's Lower East Side chose midwives as their birth attendants.[14]

Not only did Italian women use the services of midwives; the midwives themselves were also Italian immigrant women. According to a study conducted by Eugene Declerq of midwifery practices in Lawrence, Massachusetts, Italians, more than any other immigrants, attended women from their own ethnic background.[15] Similar patterns emerge in Milwaukee,[16] where Italian midwife Pasqua Cefalu delivered 97 percent of her patients in the Third Ward, where she lived. Luisa Giordano, another Italian midwife in Wisconsin, attended 422 confinement cases, and only 2 of them were non-Italians.[17] Shared ethnicity was important for both the expectant mother and the practicing midwife. They spoke the same language and shared culturally defined assumptions and traditions.

Midwives were popular with immigrant women and their families for many reasons, including an affordable price. While Milwaukee doctors were charging twenty-five dollars for a delivery, Italian midwives cost considerably less. Vincenza Bartolone, for example, recalls, "I paid the midwife [Pasqua Cefalu] five dollars for the delivery of my first child in 1920."[18]

In addition to cost, Italians, who saw childbirth as a natural event, preferred to have their babies at home and were suspicious of hospitals.[19] Like many other immigrants, they viewed home births as preferable to hospital births because the home and family life was not disturbed.[20] Conclusions drawn about midwives, especially immigrant midwives, have ignored their varied backgrounds and differing levels of education and training.[21]

According to Dye, in the early decades of the twentieth century the United States saw little in the way of a tradition of professional midwifery.[22] Midwives were described by male physicians as "filthy and ignorant and not far removed from the jungles of Africa," "relics of barbarism," and "old grannies with mouths full of snuff, fingers full of dirt and brains full of arrogance and superstition."[23] With such negative attitudes toward midwives, it is even more striking that the Italian midwives in this study were educated and professionally trained.

Current assessments also reflect misperceptions about midwives as well as inappropriate methods of analyses used to examine their working lives. One study of midwives in New York City characterizes the typical Italian midwife as a married woman and the mother of several children. Angela Danzi writes that midwifery was an acceptable way for a woman to supplement the family income. Furthermore, she states that while a small number of formally trained Italian midwives immigrated to the United States, the vast majorities were without formal education.[24]

Charlotte Borst, a historian who examined German and U.S.-born midwives in Wisconsin, similarly characterizes midwifery as "a traditional woman's occupation practiced around the needs of families and communities." She suggests that midwives, like women who took in boarders, "could adjust their job schedule to meet the needs of their families, taking fewer cases if they needed the time at home and taking more cases if they needed the extra money." Borst also concludes that midwives did not incorporate a professional ethos where the occupation itself took precedence over the needs of its practitioners. In the case of midwives, their familial responsibilities took precedence over their occupation.[25]

The assumption that women's domestic values determined entirely the relations of professionally trained midwives to their work ignores the seriousness with which professionally trained midwives conducted their practice. My examination of Italian midwives in Wisconsin leads me to very different conclusions about the professional commitment of immigrant midwives who practiced in the early decades of the twentieth century.

Because they have been categorically labeled as uneducated and ill trained, midwives are often categorized as another segment of working-class women who, as Danzi and Borst argue, worked around their family's needs. Yet, the women under review were educated and saw midwifery as a career, not simply a job. They also share other common characteristics: All were born in Italy and began practicing midwifery soon after their arrival in the United States. Each woman chose midwifery as a profession at a young age, and, moreover, some of them exhibited patterns of independent behavior not often observed among working-class Italian women.

In order to gain a greater understanding of midwifery practices in Wisconsin, I also refer to examples of Italian-born midwives who practiced in Kenosha, Wisconsin, a city just south of Milwaukee, with a fairly substantial Italian population.

The female professionals included Anna Costarella[26] and Rosa Sperandandio,[27] both of whom graduated from the Royal University of Palermo (in 1880 and 1900, respectively), while Luisa Giordano was educated at the University of Turin.[28] In 1915, Margherita Ciotti graduated from the University of the Camerino,[29] while Rosa Cesario graduated from the Medical University of Naples.[30] The only practicing Italian midwife in southeastern Wisconsin who had not been formally trained in Italy was Pasqua Cefalu, who was trained by her mother in Porticello, Sicily, but later received professional training in Milwaukee.[31] Several other midwives—Angela Cortellitti, Orsola Casoria, and Rosa DeStefano—were formally trained but not formally educated.[32] Rosa DeStefano received practical experience at the University of the Camerino in Naples, earning her certificate to practice midwifery on 15 July 1883.[33]

No doubt there were scores of immigrant midwives practicing in the early twentieth century who had little or no professional training. Still, Italian midwives in Wisconsin challenge the assumption that all immigrant midwives were poorly trained. There is also evidence that professionally trained Italian midwives were practicing in other cities. According to a New York State study, one supervisory nurse praised the Italian immigrant midwives with whom she worked as "well-educated, thoroughly trained and scientific women," adding that "in Italy none but a well-educated woman can qualify for the training, which covers from two to four years."[34]

Several cities and states regulated midwifery through licensing, which helped ensure the quality of midwifery services. The state of Wisconsin was one of only six states and the District of Columbia that required a midwife be trained for licensure by 1913.[35]

Education and training, along with regulation in various cities and states, held midwives to rigorous standards. When the practice of midwifery was attacked by the medical profession, the distinction between cities and states that regulated midwifery and those that did not were often ignored. Many critics simply assumed that all midwives lacked training and thus delivered deleterious care. For those who bothered to examine the data, however, the evidence weighs heavily in favor of the quality of care provided by midwives.

In Italy, as in most European countries, high-quality midwifery schools, usually associated with a lying-in hospital and a clinic of a university medical department, offered the latest instruction in obstetrical science.[36] Midwives learned anatomy, physiology, and elementary pathology as well as practical midwifery, often training alongside medical students. When Margherita Ciotti entered the University of the Camerino in 1914, her primary textbook was a manual of obstetrics written by highly respected doctors and professors from the universities of Pavia, Rome, and Florence.[37] The nearly five-hundred-page manual clearly illustrated every aspect of pregnancy and delivery, from the anatomy of the pregnant woman to the delivery of multiple births to instructions for performing episiotomies. A chief midwife instructor who typically offered a separate midwifery theory course often taught students. To graduate, a pupil midwife took an oral exam in front of her teacher and the members of a government commission.[38]

Successful midwifery applicants were expected not only to be educated but also to be women of good character. As in America, where hospital superintendents maintained strict control over students' work and social lives,[39] the behavior of a student midwife in Italy was subject to moral regulation. When Margherita Ciotti attended the University of the Camerino, she lived in town, close to the university, and with a family who exercised parental authority while she was a student. Another midwife, Rosa Cesario, was a student at the University of Naples. While there she lived in a convent with the Sacred Heart Nuns, who escorted female students to their classes and back to the convent by horse and carriage.[40]

According to Borst, the average midwife in Wisconsin was an older, mature woman, and her research suggested that both American and German-born women began midwifery at about age forty-eight. By contrast, Italian-born midwives in Wisconsin began formal training at the age of eighteen and began practicing in their early twenties. That midwifery was indeed a career that Italian women took seriously is suggested by the dates appearing on their applications for licensing. They allowed no time to lapse after their arrival in America before resuming midwifery. All the Italian midwives in Wisconsin registered within a few months of their arrival in the United States. Pasqua Cefalu arrived in Milwaukee during the summer of 1900 with her husband and three children. The following October she registered with the Milwaukee Public Health Department.[41] Luisa Giordano migrated to Wisconsin in 1907 and delivered her first baby one year later. Rosa Cesario and her husband immigrated to America in the spring of 1922. On 16 June 1922, Rosa registered with the Wisconsin Board of Medical Examiners to practice midwifery.[42] Margherita Ciotti had practiced midwifery for eight years in

Montemonaco, Italy, and had already attended seven hundred women prior to emigrating in 1923. In December she applied for a midwifery license.[43]

In 1909, Wisconsin legislation required that midwives be licensed. That did not prevent any of the Italian midwives from continuing their practice. Pasqua Cefalu would have been the one midwife threatened by the legislation since she did not have the formal training required under Wisconsin law. In addition she had already been practicing midwifery for thirty-two years and thus might also have considered retiring. However, at the age of fifty-two, Pasqua Cefalu enrolled in the Wisconsin School of Midwifery. She graduated and received her Wisconsin license on 15 January 1910 and continued her practice for two more decades.

Practices and Rituals of Childbirth

Ethnic patterns of midwifery practice dominated Milwaukee during the late nineteenth and early twentieth centuries. According to Borst, in 1904, for example, 53 percent of all of Milwaukee's babies were delivered by midwives, most of them in immigrant neighborhoods.[44] German midwives tended German women, and Polish midwives tended Polish women, whereas Italian midwives tended Italian women.[45] Most of the Italian midwives who attended Italian births lived in the same neighborhood as or in close proximity to the women they assisted.[46] Midwife Pasqua Cefalu delivered 87 percent of her patients in the neighborhoods of the Third Ward. For Italians, midwife-assisted births followed a tradition where women were in control and centered on the involvement and networking of females. Judy Leavitt writes that "birth was a woman's event and women sought the company of female friends and relatives to be with them through their ordeal. The psychological comforts women could provide for each other could not be matched."[47] In his novel *Christ in Concrete,* Pietro di Donato describes the female presence in the birthing room of an Italian woman in the Bronx. As the recently widowed Annunziata gives birth to a son, her brother, who hears the cries of the newborn child became childishly eager to enter the bedroom. He opened the door timidly and peeked in. "'Away! Away!' admonished the midwife. 'This is not territory for men.'"[48] Danzi's study suggests that, in home births attended by midwives, Italian women were heavily dependent on an older generation of women for ideas about birth.[49] Women learned about midwives with good reputations and could locate them by tapping into neighborhood and kinship networks.[50] These networks not only influenced the choice of a midwife but also played a central role in the delivery.

Female kin assisted during childbirth in a number of ways. Medical anthropologist Nancy Triolo's insightful look at midwives in western Sicily describes the collaboration between female kin and the attending midwife:

> Women still gave birth in the crouching position and were attended by numerous female relatives. The room where the birth took place was usually crowded with women, two of whom held the pregnant woman's knees apart, another who supported her back, and the rest who provided backup relief. A midwife knelt in front of the woman in order to receive the baby who, upon being born, was given to another attendant who washed and swaddled it.

Triolo explains that even after the prone birth position had become established throughout Sicily, reducing the need for many birth attendants, women were still attended by their mothers and sisters before, after, and—if the midwife permitted—during the birth.[51]

Italian families in Wisconsin adopted similar practices. Carolyn Pontillo, who migrated from Cosenza, Italy, to Kenosha, Wisconsin, in 1915, called for her female relatives when she was ready to give birth. Italian-born midwife Luisa Giordano routinely asked the women in attendance to help her with the delivery by, for example, putting the water on to boil and fetching the clean sheets. After the birth of her daughter, Pontillo recalls, "female relatives remained to care for the other children, prepare meals and do household chores."[52]

Italian women whose babies were delivered by midwives shared stories about their childbirth experiences and recalled the flurry of activities that took place when birth was about to begin. The husband was sent to summon the midwife and escort her to the home where his wife was about to give birth. The man and children would be driven away from the woman's bedroom, sometimes even from the house. Rose Carini, a Sicilian immigrant who lived in Milwaukee's Third Ward, recalled the day her sister was born: "*Zza* Pasqua sent us children out of the house when it was time for my mother to deliver. After the baby was born, and not until it was all bathed and cleaned, and fully dressed, were the children allowed to come back into the house."[53]

As a rule, Italian midwives did not remain in the home of the parturient woman and engage in domestic activities. In 1906, Elisabeth Crowell noted that Italian midwives in New York City left the household chores for members of the family, "not considering it part of their duties as midwives."[54]

Immigrant women in Wisconsin similarly noted that the Italian midwives who had attended them had also refrained from domestic activities, which in turn, reinforced the need to be surrounded and supported by female kin and also underscored the professional ethos shared by Wisconsin's Italian midwives.[55]

Midwives returned to the home of the parturient woman for seven to ten days following delivery. After Carolyn Pontillo gave birth to her daughter, she recalls that Giordano "returned to my home every day for one week to bathe and check the baby and to examine me for infection." She also advised her what to eat and what activities she could engage in.[56] Margherita Ciotti would visit the parturient woman for one week, bathe the baby, and take care of the mother. Ciotti paid particular attention to the mother, checking her for infection and instructing her on breastfeeding.[57]

While the midwife's primary responsibilities revolved around the birth of a child, Italian midwives often became involved with their patients before delivery. Since prenatal care was almost unheard of at the turn of the century, it was not unusual for Luisa Giordano, who practiced in Kenosha from 1908 to 1932, to meet with an expectant woman, give her a complete examination, and determine her date of delivery. Normally, she would not see the pregnant woman again until she went into labor, unless something irregular occurred during the pregnancy. Consultation with Giordano was held in her flat, which was arranged like a doctor's office. There, she met her patients in the privacy of her bedroom and examined them on a double bed covered with a huge, white sheet that she cleaned and sterilized following each patient's use.[58] In addition to routine checkups, Giordano also counseled women on the use of contraceptives.

Midwives were consulted about birth control, and some performed abortions.[59] Josephine Cialdini, who assisted her godmother Luisa Giordano, recalled that women came to her for all kinds of advice on birth control. "They told *Donna* Luisa all their problems. One woman said, 'if it wasn't for *Donna* Luisa I would have even more children than I already do.'"[60] Giordano showed women how to use contraceptives and reportedly performed abortions.

It is not known what kind of contraceptives Giordano recommended, but in the late nineteenth and early twentieth centuries, Italian women limited their family size by using vaginal douches and pessaries, while some resorted to abortions. Coitus interruptus and condoms were used in the United States, but it is unclear how popular these practices were among immigrant Italians. Anthropologists Peter and Jane Schneider suggest that while coitus interruptus was familiar to the artisan class, Italian peasants rarely practiced it in 1920.[61]

Triolo submits that, with the exception of abstinence, abortion was the only effective form of birth control available to women in Sicily and may have been practiced a long time there. Abortion techniques familiar to Sicilian women included hot or cold baths and douches, strenuous exercise, and swaddling bands wrapped tightly around the waist. Herbal infusions also helped a woman terminate a pregnancy.[62] In Milwaukee women "who were desperate from so many pregnancies,"[63] or an occasional unmarried young woman who found herself pregnant, sought help from Orsola Casoria, a Sicilian-born midwife known for her abortionist activities. In Kenosha, Luisa Giordano was deeply resented by the other midwives for performing abortions because "she made a lot of money from it."[64]

Italian women in America had to make decisions about family size, and there is evidence that "while immigrants had, on the whole, higher birth rates than native-born Americans, the birth rate of all immigrants fell in relation to their length of residence in the country."[65] Italian demographer Massimo Livi-Bacci reports that the fertility rates of Italian immigrant women had actually fallen below those of native-born white women by 1936, concluding, "The immigrants rather quickly conformed to American reproductive behavior."[66] Research conducted by John Briggs of Italian women in Rochester, New York, resulted in a similar conclusion. Italian women in Rochester did not achieve the marital fertility that the women in their home village did. Briggs suggests that Italian immigrant women were thus controlling family size to a greater extent than was the case in Italy.[67]

According to Carmelina Verrico, who lives in the southern Italian village of Santi Cosma e Damiano, "midwives were highly respected in village life; they were women of high standing."[68] Throughout Italy and Sicily, lay midwives, as well as professionally trained midwives, occupied an important position in village life.

In America, as in Italy, midwives earned a special place in the families they assisted. According to Sicilian writer Giuseppe Pitre, "the midwife becomes the *comare* to the children they delivered, a form of respect and recognition that remained with them throughout their lives."[69]

Italian midwives also played an important role in the formal presentation of the child to the community. It was the midwife, not the parents or godparents, who introduced the child to the community, carrying it to and from the church for the christening on its first public appearance. Pitre observes that the midwife in Sicily, leading the baptismal procession, carried the child and introduced it to the community.[70] Anthropologist Charlotte Gower-Chapman recalls a similar practice in Milocca, Sicily. The midwife, she reports, "is customarily a participant in the baptismal service. She takes no part in the ritual, but carries the child to the font, and after placing it in the arms of the godfather, stands to aid the priest. It is she who removes the child's cap at the proper moment."[71] In the village of Santi Cosma e Damiano, for example, elderly villagers recall the local *ostetrica* (midwife) being summoned and brought in by a donkey to act as *comare* to the child she had delivered and was now having baptized in church.[72] In Milwaukee, where the majority of Italians were Sicilian, rituals similar to those described in Sicily were followed. Pasqua Cefalu's grandson, Robert Sorci, recalls that "on christening day, my grandmother routinely went to the homes of the babies she had delivered, dressed them in their christening gowns and carried them to the church, walking proudly beside parents and godparents."[73] The midwife's participation in this religious ritual attested to her unique position in the community.

In interviews conducted with families in Wisconsin, Italian midwives are still referred to with respect and terms of endearment. Pasqua Cefalu is still known to the Italians in Milwaukee as *Zza* Pasqua (meaning "aunt" in the Sicilian dialect), while Luisa Giordano and Rosa Cesario are referred to as *Donna* Luisa and *Donna* Rosa, an Italian term of respect accorded to women of significant social standing.

Italian midwives served an important role in the life of the immigrant community. They carried on a cultural tradition where women were in control. That these were career women did not mean they did not face enormous difficulty negotiating demands of family and profession. This was especially true of married women and those with children, yet their occasional willingness to place career above family is striking. Margherita Ciotti, for example, found it extremely difficult to balance marriage and children with her career, and her decisions were significantly influenced by her professional commitments. When her husband decided to emigrate in 1920, Margherita chose to remain in Italy and continue practicing midwifery. Three years later she joined her husband in America, where she gave birth to four children over the next few years and also ran a limited practice. According to her daughters, Margherita was discontented with life in the United States, and in 1929 she left her husband in Wisconsin and with her four children returned to Italy, where she resumed midwifery in her hometown of Montemonaco. In 1933, she decided to leave her children in Italy with her sister and rejoin her husband in Wisconsin. Once again, she resumed her career as a midwife in Kenosha. Margherita did not see her children again until 1947, when she returned to Italy. A year later, she and her grown children came back to Kenosha, where they were finally reunited as a family. While Italian men frequently made numerous trips back and forth to Italy, it was not as common for Italian women to do so. It was even less common for Italian women to leave their children for considerable periods of time. Ciotti did both. The one thing that remained constant for her was midwifery. Whether in Italy or the United States, with her husband or with her children, Margherita Ciotti practiced her profession.

Rosa Cesario was another midwife who made choices that did not always conform to the usual patterns associated with Italian immigrant women. In June 1922, when she was twenty-five years old, Cesario received her certificate of registration from the Wisconsin Board of Medical Examiners. After only a year in Wisconsin, her husband, Fiorino, became ill and was advised by his doctor to return to the warmer climate of Italy. Rosa, however, chose not to leave her practice in Kenosha. She told her husband to return to Italy himself, and she lived alone in a rented apartment in the Italian section of town. In 1927, she returned to Italy to be with her dying mother. Only then did she return to her husband in Cosenza, resuming midwifery there.[74]

Orsola Casoria, a native of Sicily, was trained as a midwife in a hospital in Messina. On 30 June 1914, shortly after her arrival in Milwaukee, she received her license to practice in Wisconsin.[75] Casoria practiced midwifery in Milwaukee for nearly fifty years. This career is all the more remarkable, since in 1937 Casoria was charged with second-degree manslaughter in connection with an abortion she performed on a woman who died of peritonitis. Casoria was found guilty and was sentenced to six years in Taycheedah prison.[76] Her profession as a midwife might well have ended there, but, undaunted, Casoria reapplied for a license and continued practicing until the 1960s, when she was in her late seventies.

Oral interviews with friends and families of midwives suggest a degree of independent behavior not often observed among Italian immigrant women. While most Italian women immigrated to America as part of family groups, most commonly as wives or daughters, women who were trained as midwives often migrated alone to America. Luisa Giordano was one of those women. At the age of twenty-one she migrated to Wisconsin, where she lived alone in an upper flat, free from familial supervision and proudly advertising her profession on a black sign with gold letters: "ITALIAN AMERICAN MIDWIFE— DONNA LUISA." Italian Americans remember her as "a very educated, very professional woman." Several people interviewed discreetly added that *Donna* Luisa had "a lot of lovers but was never interested in marriage."[77]

Several of the Italian midwives in this study also exhibited independent behavior by regularly using their birth names instead of their married names. Although married to Joseph Sorci, Pasqua Cefalu was listed as such in the Milwaukee City Directories. She advertised under the name Cefalu, registered with the Milwaukee Public Health Department under the name Cefalu, and received her Wisconsin license under the name Cefalu. Only after retiring from midwifery did she begin using her married name. Margherita Ciotti also used her birth name while practicing midwifery. Her married name was Valeri, but she too appeared in city directories as Ciotti and was licensed and signed birth certificates under the name Ciotti. The practice of using birth names instead of their married names reinforces the view of these midwives as professionals.

The Decline of Midwifery

After 1920, the tradition of midwife-assisted births in the United States was in decline. By the early 1930s, midwifery practice was coming to an end. Wisconsin midwives ended their careers for a variety of reasons. Rosa Cesario returned to Italy in the late 1920s and became the head midwife of an ONMI Clinic established by Mussolini's fascist government.[78] After twenty-four years of delivering babies, Luisa Giordano gave up her practice in 1932 and retired to northern Italy. Margherita Ciotti ended her practice in the mid-1930s when second-generation Italian American women began having their babies in the hospital. Pasqua Cefalu and Orsola Casoria served a dwindling population but practiced midwifery until they were in their seventies.

Midwifery came to an end in the 1930s as a consequence of the professionalization of obstetrics and gynecology, the rapid growth of hospitals after 1920, immigration restrictions, which drastically reduced the number of immigrants, and the acceptance of American medical practices by immigrant women. While midwives were an important link with Italian cultural practices for the immigrant generation, second-generation Italian women preferred to have their babies in hospitals attended by a physician, an indication of their assimilation to American medical practices. The transition from home births with midwives to hospital births with physicians ended the careers of Italian midwives. While it lasted, however, midwifery provided many Italian women with a profession, economic independence, and status within the Italian community.

An examination of Italian midwives in Wisconsin suggests that domestic values did not necessarily or entirely shape immigrant women's work experiences in the early twentieth century. At an early age, these women made a decision to become midwives and were educated and professionally trained. Midwives were not working-class women who labored primarily as a means of earning extra money to contribute to the family economy. They did not practice midwifery because it fit in with the rhythms of daily life. If anything, midwifery had a rhythm that could not be controlled. Italian midwives in Wisconsin were women who defined themselves in terms of their education and training as professionals. They are another example of Italian women of the immigrant generation who carved out a special niche for themselves within their ethnic community and defined that world according to gender, career, and domestic values.

Epilogue

IN 1977, the *Binghamton Sunday Press* published an article on the dramatic changes that had taken place in Endicott's Italian community during the last forty years. When asked about his Italian employees, Johnson's son, George W., told the *Press*, "Their ma and pa worked for me. And then they go and work for IBM."[1]

Shoe workers of the immigrant generation were loyal to George F. Johnson and the Endicott Johnson Corporation, but increasingly, second-generation Italians looked for employment opportunities elsewhere. Endicott Johnson retained the loyalty of Italian workers largely because of welfare practices and the role that Johnson played in the lives of immigrants and their families in Endicott.

During the early years of the Depression, as the company experienced gradual decline, Johnson's efforts kept large numbers of workers employed, while he continued to provide welfare services to his employees. As the Depression worsened, however, it became more and more difficult to keep men and women employed, even with reduced hours. Shoe orders declined dramatically, and management began cutting wages and benefits, including medical services. In 1936, corporation sales and profits declined and continued to do so until 1 February 1938, when full-time salaried workers were asked to accept a 20 percent salary reduction and factory workers' wages were cut by 10 percent.[2] In 1934, Johnson gave up his yearly salary of fifty thousand dollars to contribute to the Relief Fund, which aided workers who were disabled, sick, or especially hard hit because of the Depression.[3]

In 1948, George F. Johnson passed away, and the personal touch that employees had come to expect passed with him. During the late 1950s and early 1960s, the company began to experience serious financial crisis and cut back operations. The decline continued until the corporation was sold in 1969.

The Endicott Johnson Corporation had changed dramatically from the early years of George F. Johnson's leadership. Several former employees maintained that the company started to go downhill as soon as George F. passed away. "Things weren't the same anymore. No one treated the workers like 'Daddy George' did."[4] Johnson's policies of cultivating close ties between working-class families and the corporation kept many daughters and sons tied to the concept of the "E-J Happy Family of Workers," but other second-generation Italians began to seek employment options beyond the factory.

The most important shift in female employment patterns, for all women beginning in the 1920s, was the result of a structural transformation of the economy in expanding white-collar work and the increasing demands for women in office and secretarial employment. Beginning in World War II and continuing throughout the postwar years, women continued to gain jobs in offices and clerical work. Female professions in the fields of nursing, social work, and teaching, as well as the growth of nonprofessional service enterprises such as food service and beauty shops, also drew increasing numbers of women into the workforce.[5]

Equally important were the higher educational levels of Italian women. Increasing economic improvement made it possible for Italian parents to keep daughters in school longer, a practice that was taking place nationwide. Higher levels of educational attainment among the second generation also reflected a change in attitudes and a new belief in the value of a high school education among Italian immigrants, as Miriam Cohen discovered in her study of Italians in New York City.[6] Immigrant daughters who remained in secondary schools were trained in typing, shorthand, and bookkeeping, preparing them for white-collar employment, which, since 1940, increasingly depended on a high school diploma.

In Endicott a sizeable number of immigrant daughters gained employment at Endicott Johnson, not only as factory operatives as their mothers had been, but in offices and salesrooms, where they worked as clerks, typists, and stenographers.

The generation of young people in the 1940s and beyond sought occupations that reflected their higher educational levels. Italian American women who were graduates of business school moved into careers as "IBM'ers." As Endicott Johnson fell upon hard times, IBM, with headquarters in Endicott, came into good times. The children and grandchildren of Italian immigrants who had dipped cowhides and stitched soles in the shoe factories found cleaner and more prestigious work at IBM.

In Milwaukee several shifts occurred in Italian women's employment: in factory labor, in business establishments, and in white-collar and professional jobs. By the early 1940s, Italian women's wage earning changed from domestic labor in the home to factory labor. In 1940, over 1,600 Italian women and their daughters worked outside their homes in Milwaukee. Many of these women were employed in garment factories that had recently located in the Third Ward, such as Cohen Brothers and David Adler and Sons.

While the immigrant generation of women in Milwaukee's Third Ward had employed a number of strategies for connecting the home and workplace, these opportunities were no longer available to their daughters. With the imposition of immigration restrictions in the 1920s, the number of Italians migrating to Milwaukee had been drastically reduced, and the need for boarding services provided by immigrant women nearly ended. NRA Codes in the mid-1930s outlawed homework,[7] and the establishment of retail grocery stores put many small front-room groceries out of business. While the immigrant generation of female entrepreneurs had been clustered largely in food establishments, their American-born daughters branched out into other business ventures, such as owning and operating beauty salons, gift shops, real-estate agencies, and photography studios.

As a further sign of second-generation assimilation, the transition from home births with midwives to hospital births with doctors signaled the end of midwifery. Hospital births marked the end of female control over childbirth and left immigrant women to face birth alone, without the support of female kin or friends.

While many traditional ways of earning income were ending for women of the immigrant generation, new opportunities were evolving for women of the second generation. Many of these opportunities were a result of higher levels of educational attainment among the second generation. Most important, they reflect an increasing realization among Italian parents of the value of an education. Elsie DeGhera's immigrant parents encouraged her to stay in school. "They insisted we go through high school and get our diplomas," she stated during an interview. Elsie graduated from high school and took a job as a teletype operator and, later, in an office.[8]

Italian American women who graduated high school in Milwaukee were hired as typists, stenographers, telephone operators, dental assistants, and commercial artists. In addition, some women attended college and became teachers, nurses, dieticians, and social workers, often returning to their Third Ward neighborhoods to work among the Italians.

Of the second-generation Italian women that I interviewed in Milwaukee, conflict with immigrant parents arose not over the issue of *attending* college, but *where* they would be allowed to attend college. Italian fathers were much more receptive to daughters being educated if they could do so while living at home. There were several institutions for higher education in Milwaukee, including Marquette University, Spencerian Business College, Milwaukee Vocational School, Alverno College (a women's college founded by the Catholic Sisters of St. Francis), and Downer College (later the University of Wisconsin–Milwaukee).

Tom Busalacchi recalls that his Sicilian parents would not allow his sister, Mary, to attend college out of town, but gave her permission to enroll in Spencerian Business College. She graduated in the 1920s, subsequently obtaining a job as the first bursar at Marquette University.[9] Grace Gagliano's experiences were similar. Born in the Sicilian village of Santo Stefano di Camastra, Grace was only seven years old when her family immigrated to Milwaukee. After attending high school, she wanted to attend Northwestern University in Chicago, but her father opposed it, stating, "You've got the best school in the world here at Marquette." Grace complied with her father's wishes, attended Marquette University in the 1930s, and was hired as a history teacher at St. John's Cathedral School.[10]

Gaetanina Balistreri's father encouraged his children to pursue a higher education as long as they remained at home. "One day my dad and I sat down and I told my dad I would like to go to college," she said. Her father thoughtfully replied, "Well, I will pay your tuition if you will get a part-time job. Naturally, you'll live at home and you'll be taken care of, but you'll have to work for your books and spending money."[11] Gaetanina remained at home and attended college in the 1940s, becoming the first person in her family to graduate from college. After several years of teaching, she attended graduate school and became a librarian. As they shaped their family lives in response to American society, immigrant parents continued to assert parental authority, but often with a spirit of compromise, allowing children to adapt to American norms within the parameters of Italian cultural traditions.

For the immigrant generation, Milwaukee's narrow employment opportunities limited Italian women's work options, but undaunted, they found productive ways to support themselves and contribute to the support and upward mobility of their families. Italian women exhibited a spirit of entrepreneurship and self-sufficiency by establishing home-based business enterprises that served the immigrant community. From the time of their arrival in Wisconsin, Italian midwives helped sustain immigrant women in their transition to life in America. All of these women carved out a special niche for themselves within their ethnic community and defined that world according to gender, career, and domestic values.

Italian immigrant women engaged in wage labor outside the home when conditions were favorable for doing so. Those conditions were determined by the economic structure of a given region, the demands of the labor market, the presence of other women—particularly family members within a given industry—and the proximity of home to workplace. In Endicott Italian women encountered favorable conditions for participating in wage labor. Immigrant women relied on cultural values to guide them in their adaptation to a new industrial environment, such as kinship networks that were used to secure jobs and provide childcare for working mothers. Furthermore, Endicott Johnson's program of corporate welfare, the flexibility in hours and conditions for working mothers, the aid extended to families in home buying, the medical benefits, all translated into family values—values with which immigrant women could identify.

Immigration to the United States provided Italian women with struggles and opportunities. Italian women, faced with the complexities of adapting to a new environment, transplanted skills and training acquired in Italy to urban life in America. Where Old World experiences failed to provide them with ways of organizing familial goals and economic expectations, immigrant women embraced new employment opportunities within an Italian social and cultural milieu.

The ability of immigrant women to earn income while balancing responsibilities as wives and mothers attests to Italian women's cultural and economic agency in adapting to American society. Moreover, the examples of immigrant workingwomen in Endicott and Milwaukee broaden our definition of Italian women workers in the United States. Focusing on questions of gender and women's work reveals that women's actions and identities varied considerably from those who worked solely to help support the family to those who thought of themselves as professional or career women. The range of women's work experiences revealed in this study retheorizes the dominant stereotype of passive, cloistered Italian immigrant women by recovering the lives of those women who were competitive factory laborers, shrewd businesswomen, and professional midwives.

Notes

Introduction

1. Vincenza Bartolone and Conchetta Crivello (daughters of Maria and Salvatore Latona), interview with author, Milwaukee, Wis., 20 March 1992.

2. Dolores Molinaro Wood (daughter of Bridgetta Bianco Molinaro), interview with author, Binghamton, N.Y., 30 April 1987.

3. Amy Bernardy's 1909 study of Italians in the United States was perhaps the first to associate immigrant women's work choices with intensely jealous husbands. Scholars of the Italian immigrant experience supported this argument in early works. See Amy Allemand Bernardy, "Inchiesta sulle condizioni delle donne e dei fanciuli negli state del Nordest della Confederazione Americana," *Bolletino dell'emigrazione* 1 (1909): 13; the works of Virginia Yans-McLaughlin, including *Family and Community: Italian Immigrants in Buffalo, 1880–1930* (Ithaca: Cornell University Press, 1982); "Italian Women and Work: Experience and Perception," in *Class, Sex, and the Woman Worker*, ed. Milton Cantor and Bruce Laurie (Westport, Conn.: Greenwood, 1977), 100–119; and "Patterns of Work and Family Organization: Buffalo's Italians," *Journal of Interdisciplinary History* 2 (1971): 299–314; also Barbara Klaczynska, "Why Women Work: A Comparison of Various Groups—Philadelphia, 1910–1930," *Labor History* 17 (Winter 1976): 73–87; Betty Boyd Caroli and Thomas Kessner, "New Immigrant Women at Work: Italians and Jews in New York City, 1880–1905," *Journal of Ethnic Studies* 5 (Winter 1978): 19–31; and Mary Jane Cappozzoli, *Three Generations of Italian American Women in Nassau County, 1925–1981* (New York: Garland, 1990).

4. Maddalena Tirabassi, "Bourgeois Men, Peasant Women: Rethinking Domestic Work and Morality in Italy," in *Women, Gender, and Transnational Lives: Italian Workers of the World*, ed. Donna Gabaccia and Franca Iacovetta (Toronto: University of Toronto Press, 2002), 106–29.

5. Ibid., 109–10.

6. Diane Vecchio, "Gender, Domestic Values, and Italian Working Women in Milwaukee: Immigrant Midwives and Businesswomen," in *Women, Gender, and Transnational Lives: Italian Workers of the World,* ed. Donna Gabaccia and Franca Iacovetta (Toronto: University of Toronto Press, 2002), 160–85.

7. Julia Kirk Blackwelder, *Now Hiring: The Feminization of Work in the United States, 1900–1995* (College Station: Texas A&M University, 1997), 71–72.

8. Contemporary studies reported that Italian women dominated the needle trades at the turn of the century. See Mabel Hurd Willet, *The Employment of Women in the Clothing Trade* (New York: Columbia University Press, 1902); Edith Abbott, *Women in Industry: A Study in American Economic History* (New York: Appleton, 1910); Louise Odencrantz, *Italian Women in Industry: A Study of Conditions in New York City* (New York: Russell Sage Foundation, 1919); and Joel Seidman, *The Needle Trades* (New York: Farrar & Rinehart, 1942).

9. Nancy Hewitt, *Southern Discomfort: Women's Activism in Tampa, Florida, 1880s-1920s* (Urbana: University of Illinois Press, 2001); and Gary R. Mormino and George E. Pozzetta, *The Immigrant World of Ybor City: Italians and Their Latin Neighbors in Tampa, 1885–1985* (Urbana: University of Illinois Press, 1987), 108. According to Mormino and Pozzetta, 40 percent of all Italian-born women in Ybor City were employed in the cigar factories.

10. Vicki Ruiz, *Cannery Women, Cannery Lives: Mexican Women, Unionization, and the California Food Processing Industry, 1930–1950* (Albuquerque: University of New Mexico, 1987).

11. Donna Gabaccia and Franca Iacovetta, "Women, Work, and Protest in the Italian Diaspora: An International Research Agenda," *Labour/Le Travail* 42 (Fall 1998): 161–81.

12. Willet, *Employment of Women,* 36.

13. Cynthia Daniels, "No Place Like Home: Homeworkers of New York, 1900–1914" (unpublished paper). Much of Daniels's work referred to here was later published in a slightly different form in Eileen Boris and Cynthia Daniels, *Homework: Historical and Contemporary Perspectives on Paid Labor at Home* (Urbana: University of Illinois Press, 1989).

14. John Modell and Tamara K. Hareven, "Urbanization and the Malleable Household: An Examination of Boarding and Lodging in American Families," *Journal of Marriage and the Family* 35 (August 1973): 467–79.

15. Alice Kessler-Harris, *Out to Work: A History of Wage-Earning Women in the United States* (Oxford: Oxford University Press, 1982), 125.

16. Judith Smith, *Family Connections: A History of Italian and Jewish Immigrant Lives in Providence, Rhode Island, 1900–1940* (Albany: State University of New York Press, 1985), 48.

17. Nancy Foner, *From Ellis Island to JFK: New York's Two Great Waves of Immigration* (New Haven, Conn.: Yale University Press, 2000), 117.

18. Donna Gabaccia, *From the Other Side: Women, Gender, and Immigrant Life in the U.S., 1820–1990* (Bloomington: Indiana University Press, 1994), 56.

19. Fran Leeper Buss, *La Partera: Story of a Midwife* (Ann Arbor: University of Michigan Press, 1993). Many stories about Mexican American midwives are recounted in Patricia Preciado Martin, *Songs My Mother Sang to Me: An Oral History of Mexican American Women* (Tucson: University of Arizona Press, 1992).

20. Louise Tilly, "Urban Growth, Industrialization, and Women's Employment in Milan, Italy, 1881–1911," *Journal of Urban History* 3.4 (August 1977): 467–84.

21. There are other aspects of immigrant women's lives that I chose not to include in this study. For example, Italian women in Endicott and Milwaukee were involved in relief work and charitable activities and joined church organizations and mutual aid societies. While these important activities shed light on gender and community activism, they were not directly connected to women's work or the workplace in either Endicott or Milwaukee.

22. In the early 1970s when the Endicott Johnson Corporation started to fold and factory buildings were being destroyed, historian Luciano Iorizzo (SUNY Oswego) salvaged employment records from the Endicott offices. Of these, 475 employment records were of Italian women workers. These records are currently held by Gerald Zahavi (SUNY Albany).

23. Anthropologist Diane Wolf discusses insider/outsider privileges in conducting oral research, asserting that "those who studied a group to which they belonged often claimed to have an advantage that led to a privileged or more balanced view of the people/society under study." At the same time, however, outsiders report that informants were more likely to offer other kinds of information that may not be shared with an insider. See Diane Wolf, ed., *Feminist Dilemmas in Fieldwork* (Boulder, Colo.: Westview, 1996); see also Daphne Patai and Sherna Gluck, eds., *Women's World: The Feminist Practice of Oral History* (New York: Routledge, 1991).

Prologue

1. Alex Vecchio (son of Emilia Palazzo), interview with author, Skaneateles Lake, N.Y., 6 July 2000.

2. See Yans-McLaughlin, *Family and Community*; Miriam Cohen, *Workshop to Office: Two Generations of Italian Women in New York City, 1900–1950* (Ithaca: Cornell University Press, 1992); and Smith, *Family Connections*.

3. Joan Scott and Louise Tilly, "Women's Work and the Family in Nineteenth-Century Europe," *Comparative Studies in Society and History* 18 (1975): 36–64.

4. Tirabassi, "Bourgeois Men, Peasant Women," 109–10.

5. Ibid., 110–11.

6. Elda Gentili Zappi, *If Eight Hours Seem Too Few: Mobilization of Women Workers in the Italian Rice Fields* (Albany: State University of New York Press, 1991), 9.

7. *Matrimonio* Records, 1936, Comune de Santi Cosma e Damiano, Italy.

8. Emiliana P. Noether, "The Silent Half: *Le Contadine del Sud* before the First World War," in *The Italian Immigrant Woman in North America: Proceedings of the Tenth Annual Conference of the American Italian Historical Association*, ed. Betty Boyd Caroli, Robert Harney, and Lydio Tomasi (Toronto: Multicultural History Society of Ontario, 1978), 3–12.

9. Rudolph Bell, *State and Honor: Family and Village Demographic and Cultural Change in Rural Italy since 1800* (Chicago: University of Chicago Press, 1979), 121–23.

10. According to Noether, "Silent Half," 7, women worked in large numbers alongside men, a fact brought out by figures in a 1902 government report.

11. Erasmo Falso, *Ventosa: Antico Paese del Sud*, Archives, Comune de Santi Cosma e Damiano, Italy.

12. Kathie Friedman-Kasaba, *Memories of Migration: Gender, Ethnicity, and Work in the Lives of Jewish and Italian Women in New York, 1870–1925* (Albany: State University of New York Press, 1996), 76.

13. Marie Hall Ets, *Rosa: The Life of an Italian Immigrant* (Minneapolis: University of Minnesota, 1970; reprinted Madison: University of Wisconsin Press, 1999), 75.

14. Tilly, "Urban Growth."

15. Simonetta Ortaggi Cammarosano, "Labouring Women in Northern and Central Italy in the Nineteenth Century," in *Society and Politics in the Age of the Risorgimento: Essays in Honor of Denis Mack Smith*, ed. John A. Davis and Paul Ginsborg (New York: Cambridge University Press, 1991), 152–83.

16. Pierfrancesco Bandettini, "The Employment of Women in Italy, 1881–1951," *Comparative Studies in Society* 2 (1959–60): 369–74.

17. Linda Reeder, *Widows in White: Migration and the Transformation of Rural Italian Women, Sicily, 1880–1920* (Toronto: University of Toronto Press, 2003), 161.

18. Columbia Furio, "The Cultural Background of the Italian Immigrant Woman and Its Impact on Her Unionization in the New York City Garment Industry, 1880–1919," in *Pane e Lavoro: The Italian American Working Class: Proceedings of the American Italian Historical Association*, ed. George Pozetta (Toronto: Multicultural Historical Society of Ontario, 1980), 81–97.

19. Lucia Chiavola Birnbaum, *Liberazione della Donna: Feminism in Italy* (Middleton, Conn.: Wesleyan University Press, 1986), 14–16.

20. Tirabassi, "Bourgeois Men, Peasant Women," 112.

21. Ibid., 113.

22. Victoria DeGrazia, *How Fascism Ruled Women: Italy, 1920–1945* (Berkeley: University of California Press, 1992), 65.

23. Nancy Triolo, "The Angelmakers: Fascist Pro-Natalism and the Normalization of Midwives in Sicily" (Ph.D. diss., University of California at Berkeley, 1989).

24. Reeder, *Widows in White*, 160.

25. Tirabassi, "Bourgeois Men, Peasant Women," 112–13.

26. *Matrimonio* Records, Comune de Santi Cosma e Damiano, Italy.

27. Carmelina Verrico, interview with author, Santi Cosma e Damiano, Italy, April 2000. *Possidente* were large landowners.

28. Tirabassi also points out that peasant women's work in Italy has failed to penetrate immigration literature; see "Bourgeois Men, Peasant Women," 108.

29. Odencrantz, *Italian Women in Industry*, 27–28.

30. Employment records, Endicott Johnson Corporation.

31. Paola Corti, "Women Were Labour Migrants Too: Tracing Late-Nineteenth-Century Female Migration from Northern Italy to France," in *Women, Gender, and Transnational Lives: Italian Workers of the World,* ed. Donna Gabaccia and Franca Iacovetta (Toronto: University of Toronto Press, 2002), 133–59.

Chapter 1: Encountering America

1. Catherine Balistreri (daughter of Catherine D'Acquisto Dentice), interview with author, Milwaukee, Wis., 23 March 1991.

2. Endicott Johnson employment card for Amelia Bertoni.

3. Samuel Baily, *Immigrants in the Lands of Promise: Italians in Buenos Aires and New York City, 1870–1914* (New York: Cornell University Press, 1999).

4. Friedman-Kasaba, *Memories of Migration,* 74.

5. Reports of the Immigration (Dillingham) Commission, *Occupations of the First and Second Generations of Immigrants in the United States* (Washington, D.C.: Government Printing Office, 1911), 169.

6. Kessler-Harris, *Out to Work,* 121.

7. William Seward Foote, *Binghamton and Broome County, New York: A History* (Binghamton, N.Y.: Historical Publishing, 1924).

8. Gerald Zahavi, *Workers, Managers, and Welfare Capitalism: The Shoeworkers and Tanners of Endicott Johnson, 1890–1950* (Urbana: University of Illinois Press, 1988), 2–3.

9. Ibid., 4.

10. Jeffrey Pines, "Endicott, New York: Industry, Immigrants and Paternalism" (Master's thesis, State University of New York at Binghamton, 1982), 10.

11. Kathleen Neils Conzen, *Immigrant Milwaukee, 1836–1860: Accommodation and Community in a Frontier City* (Cambridge: Harvard University Press, 1976), 15–18.

12. John Gurda, *The Making of Milwaukee* (Milwaukee: Milwaukee County Historical Society, 1999), 170.

13. Bayrd Still, *Milwaukee: The History of a City* (Madison: State Historical Society of Wisconsin, 1965), 112.

14. Gerd Korman, *Industrialization, Immigrants, and Americanizers: The View from Milwaukee, 1866–1921* (Madison: State Historical Society of Wisconsin, 1967).

15. Still, *Milwaukee,* 186–88.

16. Ibid., 189.

17. Gurda, *Making of Milwaukee,* 161–62.

18. Ibid., 163–64.

19. Ibid., 120.

20. Korman, *Industrialization,* 22–23.

21. John Gurda, *Bay View, Wisconsin* (Madison: University of Wisconsin Board of Regents, 1979), 16.

22. Korman, *Industrialization,* 22–23.

23. Wisconsin Bureau of Labor and Industrial Statistics, *Biennial Report, 1885–86,* 426.

24. Louis J. Swichkow, "A Dual Heritage: The Jewish Community of Milwaukee, 1900–70" (Ph.D. diss., Marquette University, 1973), 62.

25. Ibid., 81.

26. Roger Simon, "Housing and Services in an Immigrant Neighborhood: Milwaukee's Ward 14," *Journal of Urban History* 2 (August 1976): 435–57.

27. Zahavi, *Workers, Managers, and Welfare Capitalism,* 63–65.

28. Fifteenth Census of the United States, *Population,* 1930, vol. 3, pt. 2, 299–303.

29. Marriage registration records, St. Anthony of Padua Church, Endicott, N.Y.

30. Josef Barton, *Peasants and Strangers: Italians, Rumanians, and Slovaks in an American City, 1890–1950* (Cambridge: Harvard University Press, 1975), 53–54.

31. John W. Briggs, *An Italian Passage: Immigrants to Three American Cities, 1890–1930* (New Haven: Yale University Press, 1978), 69–70. Barton's research on migration patterns in Cleveland supports this. Barton notes that the most striking feature of the Italian immigration was the predominance of large village chains. He explains that the median size of village streams was thirty persons and that fully a fourth arrived in chains of a hundred or more migrants. One-half of the Italian arrivals moved from town villages in southern Italy to major village concentrations in Cleveland. Pioneer Italian migration to Cleveland thus developed into large-scale chain migration from both villages in particular and districts in general.

32. Interview with Nancy Grey Osterud, quoted in Zahavi, *Workers, Managers, and Welfare Capitalism,* 70.

33. Frank Allio, interview with author, Endicott, N.Y., 28 May 1987.

34. Mary Monticello, interview with author, Endicott, N.Y., 23 September 1987.

35. Fifteenth Census of the United States, 1930, Number and Distribution of Inhabitants, 18.

36. George LaPiana, *Italians in Milwaukee, Wisconsin* (New York: Associated Charities, 1915), 5–6.

37. Mario Carini, *Milwaukee's Italians: The Early Years* (Milwaukee: Italian Community Center, 1999), 27.

38. Josephine Rampolla (daughter of Anna Torretta), interview with author, Milwaukee, Wis., 20 April 1991.

39. Tony DiCristo (son of Vito DiCristo), interview with author, Milwaukee, Wis., 16 March 1991.

40. Judith Simonson, "The Third Ward: Symbol of Ethnic Identity," *Milwaukee History,* Summer 1987, 61–76.

41. Carini, *Milwaukee's Italians,* 29.

42. Gurda, *Bay View,* 12.

43. Carini, *Milwaukee's Italians,* 29.

44. U.S. Senate, *Reports of the Immigration Commission: Immigrants in Cities* (Washington, D.C.: Government Printing Office, 1911), 2.546–48.

45. Korman, *Industrialization,* 28.

46. Ibid.

47. Joe William Trotter, *Black Milwaukee: The Making of an Industrial Proletariat, 1915–45* (Urbana: University of Illinois Press, 1985), 18.

48. Ross McGuire and Nancy Grey Osterud, *Working Lives: Broome County, New York, 1800–1930* (Binghamton, N.Y.: Roberson Center for the Arts and Sciences, 1980), 68.

49. Gabaccia, *From the Other Side,* 46.

50. Rudolph J. Vecoli, "Contadini in Chicago: A Critique of 'The Uprooted,'" *Journal of American History* 51 (1964): 404–17.

Chapter 2: Gender, Economic Opportunities, and Italian Women Workers in Endicott

1. *E-J Workers Review,* November 1920, 12, Broome County Historical Society Library, Roberson Center for the Arts and Sciences, Binghamton, N.Y.

2. New York State Manuscript Census, Endicott, 1925.

3. Zahavi, *Workers, Managers, and Welfare Capitalism,* 53.

4. In her analysis of women, work, and the family, Winifred Wandersee explains that "economic need is a concept not easily measured. The issue of need cuts across class lines, and although the intensity of need varies, the phenomenon is dependent upon the particular values of individual families rather than the absolute requirements of daily survival." See Wandersee, *Women's Work and Family Values, 1920–1940* (Cambridge: Harvard University Press, 1981), 1.

5. The 475 employment records represent all existing records of Italian women workers. Information provided on the employment cards includes date of hire, local residence, birth date, nativity, marital status, number of children and their ages, and the department in which a person was hired to work. My analysis of age, marital status, number of children, and so on is based on the information provided on the employment cards at the date of first hire. This information obviously changed according to the circumstances in a woman's life. Thus, at any time the actual average age or the percentage of married women working differed from the data based at the time of hire.

6. Endicott Johnson employment card for Angelina Franciscone.

7. Endicott Johnson employment card for Nicolette Fiore.

8. Endicott Johnson employment card for Grace Colonna.

9. Many young girls, such as Bridgetta Bianco, for example, had to drop out of school to help the family. Other women, such as Frances Vivona Cizanek, admitted that they went to work at an early age because they disliked school and decided to drop out.

10. Endicott Johnson employment card for Adeline Alimonti.

11. Mary Blewett, "Work, Gender, and the Artisan Tradition in New England Shoemaking, 1780–1860," *Journal of Social History* 17 (1983): 224.

12. Kessler-Harris, *Out to Work,* 144.

13. Andrea Tone, *The Business of Benevolence: Industrial Paternalism in Progressive America* (Ithaca: Cornell University Press, 1997), 154.

14. Zahavi, *Workers, Managers, and Welfare Capitalism,* 71.

15. Katie Wasylysyn Chopiak, interview with Nancy Grey Osterud, 6 August 1982, Broome County Immigration Project, quoted by Zahavi, *Workers, Managers, and Welfare Capitalism,* 71.

16. Zahavi, *Workers, Managers, and Welfare Capitalism,* 71.

17. Helen Weaver, interview with Susan Dobandi, 20 March 1978, Broome County Immigration Project.

18. Frances Vivona Cizanek, 12 April 1988; Carmela Giuliani, 12 April 1988; Elisabetta Manziano, 28 May 1987; Mary and Fred Monticello, 23 September 1987; and Rose Grassi Annis, 23 September 1987, interviews with author, Endicott, N.Y. (Giuliani's and Manziano's names have been changed to protect the privacy of the interviewees.)

19. Wood interview.

20. Annis interview.

21. Manziano interview.

22. Monticello interview.

23. Odencrantz, *Italian Women in Industry,* 179.

24. Ruiz, *Cannery Women, Cannery Lives,* 14.

25. Annis interview.

26. Cohen, *Workshop to Office,* 149.

27. Judith Smith, "Italian Mothers, American Daughters: Changes in Work and Family Roles," in *The Italian Immigrant Woman in North America: Proceedings of the Tenth Annual Conference of the AIHA,* ed. Betty Boyd Caroli, Robert F. Harney, and Lydio F. Tomasi (Toronto: Multicultural History Society of Ontario, 1978), 206–21.

28. John Bodnar's study of immigrants in Pittsburgh reveals that every Italian interviewed relied on kin or friends to persuade foremen or other supervisors to hire them. See Bodnar, "Immigration, Kinship, and the Rise of Working-Class Realism in Industrial America," *Journal of Social History* 14 (1980–81) : 45–63.

29. Ibid., 52.

30. Cizanek interview.

31. Tamara Hareven, *Family Time and Industrial Time: The Relationship between*

the Family and Work in a New England Industrial Community (New York: Cambridge University Press, 1982), 85.

32. Quoted in McGuire and Osterud, *Working Lives,* 73.

33. Manziano interview.

34. Annis interview.

35. Wood, Manziano, and Annis interviews.

36. Donna Gabaccia, *From Sicily to Elizabeth Street: Housing and Social Change among Italian Immigrants, 1880–1930* (Albany: State University of New York Press, 1984), 43.

37. Wood interview.

38. All of the people interviewed agreed that Italian families helped each other out with childcare. Where no family existed there were plenty of Italian neighbors with whom young mothers could feel secure leaving their children. Mary Monticello brought her three children to an Italian widow who "loved the children like they were her own." Monticello interview.

39. Julia Ericksen, "An Analysis of the Journey to Work for Women," *Social Problems* 24 (1977): 428–35.

40. Susan Hanson and Ibipo Johnston, "Gender Differences in Work-Trip Length: Explanation and Implications," *Urban Geography* 6 (1985): 193–219.

41. Odencrantz, *Italian Women in Industry,* 33–34.

42. Klaczynska, "Why Women Work."

43. Manziano interview.

44. Allio interview.

45. Manziano interview.

46. Zahavi, *Workers, Managers, and Welfare Capitalism,* 10–14.

47. Ibid.

48. George F. Johnson to E. D. Cook, Binghamton, N.Y., September 1925, George F. Johnson Papers, MSS 10, box 5, George F. Johnson Collection, Special Collections Research Center at Bird Library at Syracuse University, Syracuse, N.Y. (hereafter Johnson Papers).

49. Harry L. Johnson to George F. Johnson, 1 February 1917, MSS 10, box 3, Johnson Papers.

50. Anna Gimmie, interview with Michele Morrison, 30 September 1982, Broome County Immigration Project.

51. William Inglis, *George F. Johnson and His Industrial Democracy* (New York: Huntington, 1935), 140–41.

52. Monticello interview.

53. Sam Salvatore, interview with Gerald Zahavi, Binghamton, N.Y., 7 July 1981.

54. Wood interview.

55. Nikki Mandell, *The Corporation as Family: The Gendering of Corporate Welfare, 1890–1930* (Chapel Hill: University of North Carolina Press, 2002), 8.

56. Antoinette Santodonato, interview with Leora Ornstein, 25 April 1983, Broome County Immigration Project.

57. George F. Johnson to G. A. Breckinridge, 5 January 1923, MSS 10, box 7, Johnson Papers.

58. Irving Bernstein, *A History of the American Worker, 1920–1933: The Lean Years* (Boston: Houghton Mifflin, 1960), 170.

59. "An E-J Workers' First Lesson in the Square Deal," George F. Johnson Collection, Pamphlet File, Special Collections Research Center at Bird Library at Syracuse University, Syracuse, N.Y.

60. Mandell, *Corporation as Family*, 18.

61. Daniel C. O'Neill, "A Plan of Medical Service for the Industrial Worker and His Family," *Journal of the American Medical Association* 91 (17 November 1928): 1516–19.

62. Zahavi, *Workers, Managers, and Welfare Capitalism*, 48–49.

63. Report to George F. Johnson from T. H. Platt, 10 March 1929, George F. Johnson Papers, Endicott Johnson Corporation, Main Office, Endicott, N.Y.

64. Quoted in Zahavi, *Workers, Managers, and Welfare Capitalism*, 71.

65. Mandell, *Corporation as Family*, 53.

66. *E-J Workers Review*, April 1919, 25.

67. See, for example, Susan Porter Benson, *Counter Cultures: Saleswomen, Managers, and Customers in American Department Stores, 1890–1940* (Urbana: University of Illinois Press, 1986); and Susan Strom, *Beyond the Typewriter: Gender, Class, and the Origins of Modern American Office Work, 1900–1930* (Urbana: University of Illinois Press, 1992).

68. Monticello interview. Mary Monticello reported that she nursed all three children through childhood illnesses during the years she worked at Endicott Johnson. Although she did not get paid, she was grateful for having the time off to be with her children and still return to her job. She reported that foremen were kind and understanding whenever a family emergency arose.

69. Letter published in the *E-J Workers Review*, July 1919.

70. "Organized play for one thousand children is being carried out in six parks in Johnson City and Endicott under direction of the E-J Athletic Department to keep children off the streets. Before this play spot was opened, hundreds of children swarmed the streets of that section of Endicott. The children are being taught the right kind of recreation and the fairness of playing square," announced the *E-J Workers Review* in July 1923.

71. Zahavi, *Workers, Managers, and Welfare Capitalism*, 58.

72. Tone, *Business of Benevolence*, 89.

73. George Basler, "The Johnson Legacy," *The Sunday Press*, 4 September 1983.

74. Bonnie Franz, *Broome County Historical Society Newsletter*, Fall 1982.

75. Jeffrey Pines, "Endicott, New York: Immigrants, Industry, and Paternalism" (honors thesis, State University of New York at Binghamton, 1982), 42.

76. Ibid., 91.

77. George F. Johnson to Michael D. Riolo, 3 July 1919, MSS 10, box 5, Johnson Papers.

78. Analysis of Italians who purchased Endicott Johnson homes was based on an examination of twenty ledgers of the Endicott Johnson Realty Transactions between the years 1906 and 1944, Endicott Johnson Main Office, Endicott, N.Y.

79. George W. Johnson to George F. Johnson, 28 March 1935, George F. Johnson Papers, Endicott Johnson Corporation.

80. *E-J Workers Review*, February 1921.

81. Some of these new home owners included Fanny Barlotta Catalano, Mary Monaco, Martha Pinto, Lucy Rizzi, Jennie Battista, Mary Perella, Marie Puglisi, Lena Quirello, Mary Rose, Josephine Sabo, Susie Zampi, Mary Crosetto, Madeline Cucci, Mary Agresta, Katherine DiGaramo, Lucille Farrai, Teresa Demo, and Victoria Vargo, among others.

82. James Fiori, *A History of Endicott* (Endicott, N.Y.: Union Press, 1981).

83. Ledgers, Endicott Johnson Realty Transactions.

84. John Bodnar, Roger Simon, and Michael P. Weber, *Lives of Their Own: Blacks, Italians, and Poles in Pittsburgh, 1900–1960* (Urbana: University of Illinois Press, 1982), 154.

85. Yans-McLaughlin, *Family and Community*, 47–48.

86. Memorandum written by George F. Johnson (date unknown), George F. Johnson Papers, Endicott Johnson Corporation.

87. Confirmed in interviews with Monticello, Manziano, and Annis. All had experienced financial difficulties either as children of immigrant parents or themselves as young adults, working for the corporation. In all instances, they agreed that wives were the ones who approached the Personnel Office requesting aid.

88. Bonne Franz interview with a former Endicott Johnson employee (name unknown), *Broome County Historical Society Newsletter*, Fall 1982.

89. Bernstein, *American Worker*, 187.

90. Zahavi, *Workers, Managers, and Welfare Capitalism*.

91. Tone, *Business of Benevolence*, 4–7.

92. Luciano Iorizzo and Salvatore Mondello, *The Italian Americans* (New York: Twayne, 1971), 141.

93. Cizanek interview.

94. Manziano interview.

95. Monticello interview.

96. Tamara K. Hareven and Randolph Langenbach, *Amoskeag: Life and Work in an American Factory-City* (New York: Pantheon, 1978), 21.

97. McGuire and Osterud, *Working Lives*, 73.

98. Annis interview.

99. McGuire and Osterud, *Working Lives*, 75–76.

100. Wood interview.

101. Patricia R. Pessar, "The Linkage between the Household and Workplace of Dominican Women in the U.S.," *International Migration Review* 18 (Winter 1984): 1188–1211.

102. Zahavi, *Workers, Managers, and Welfare Capitalism,* 155.

103. Monticello interview.

104. Manziano interview.

105. Wood interview.

106. Cizanek interview.

107. Zahavi, *Workers, Managers, and Welfare Capitalism,* 157.

108. Ibid., 150.

109. Hareven, *Family Time,* 76–77.

110. Jacqueline Dowd Hall et al., *Like a Family: The Making of a Southern Cotton Mill World* (Chapel Hill: University of North Carolina Press, 1987), 114.

111. Interviews with Endicott Johnson employees.

112. Kathy Peiss, *Cheap Amusements: Working Women and Leisure in Turn-of-the-Century New York* (Philadelphia: Temple University Press, 1986), 45

113. As reported in the *E-J Workers Review.*

114. Helen Venturino is the young woman assisted by her uncle in gaining employment at Endicott Johnson after her husband deserted her and their infant child.

115. *E-J Workers Review,* October 1920.

116. Yans-McLaughlin writes that in 1905 only 12 percent of married Italian women from the ward with the highest Italian population were employed outside the home.

117. See Yans-McLaughlin, *Family and Community;* and "Italian Women and Work."

118. Abstract of the Fourteenth Census of the United States, 1920, 524.

119. Ibid.

Chapter 3: Gender, Economic Opportunities, and Italian Businesswomen in Milwaukee

1. Carini, *Milwaukee's Italians,* 32.

2. Ibid., 39.

3. Ibid., 44.

4. Korman, *Industrialization,* 20.

5. *Immigrants in Cities,* 2.546–48, table 401.

6. State of Wisconsin, Wisconsin Bureau of Labor Statistics, 1900–01, 644, Archives, Wisconsin State Historical Society, Madison, Wis.

7. U.S. Department of Commerce, Bureau of the Census, "Census of the Population, 1900" (Washington, D.C.: Government Printing Office).

8. U.S. Department of Commerce, Bureau of the Census, "Census of the Population, 1920" (Washington, D.C.: Government Printing Office).

9. Mario Carini, interview with author, Milwaukee, Wis., 4 March 2000.

10. *Immigrants in Cities,* 743.

11. Ibid., 735–37.

12. Ibid., 748.

13. Ewa Morawska, "The Sociology and Historiography of Immigration," in *Immigration Reconsidered: History, Sociology, and Politics,* ed. Virginia Yans-McLaughlin (New York: Oxford University Press, 1990), 187–238.

14. Donna Gabaccia, *We Are What We Eat: Ethnic Food and the Making of Americans* (Cambridge: Harvard University Press, 1998), 67.

15. Walter Nugent, *Into the West: The Story of Its People* (New York: Vintage, 2001), 163.

16. Gabaccia, *We Are What We Eat,* 75.

17. Friedman-Kasaba, *Memories of Migration,* 129.

18. Nancy Foner, "Immigrant Women and Work in New York City, Then and Now," *Journal of American Ethnic History* 18.3 (Spring 1999): 95–113.

19. For a discussion of Jewish boarding practices, see Susan A. Glenn, *Daughters of the Shtetl: Life and Labor in the Immigrant Generation* (Ithaca: Cornell University Press, 1990).

20. From the oral history of Carlotta Silvas Martin in Martin, *Songs My Mother Sang to Me,* 201.

21. Judy Yung, *Unbound Feet: A Social History of Chinese Women in San Francisco* (Berkeley: University of California Press, 1995), 78.

22. *Immigrants in Cities,* 695–717.

23. LaPiana, *Italians in Milwaukee,* 16.

24. Assunta Curri, interview with author, Cortland, N.Y., June 1985.

25. Diane Vecchio, "The Influence of Family Values and Culture on the Occupational Choices of Italian Immigrant Women in Cortland, N.Y., 1890–1935," in *From Many Roots: Immigrants and Ethnic Groups in the History of Cortland County, New York,* ed. Louis M. Vanaria (Cortland, N.Y.: Cortland County Historical Society, 1986), 38.

26. Yans-McLaughlin, *Family and Community,* 170.

27. Gabaccia, *From Sicily to Elizabeth Street,* 27–28. Gabaccia also refers to anthropologist Charlotte Gower Chapman, who reported that in Milocca boarding was unheard of.

28. Abraham Cahan, *The Rise of David Levinsky* (1917; reprinted New York: Penguin, 1993).

29. Rose Carini, interview with author, Milwaukee, Wis., 26 August 1992.

30. Marie Vecchio, interview with author, Miami, Fla., 2 January 2000.

31. Information compiled from marriage certificates and interviews.

32. Coroner's Report, Kenosha, Wis. (1911–1918), Series 43, 27 November 1911.

33. *Immigrants in Cities,* 717.

34. Paul Geib, "From Italian Peddler to Commission Row Wholesaler," *Milwaukee History,* Winter 1990, 102–12.

35. Franca Bellardini, interview with author, Milwaukee, Wis., 4 May 1993. (The name has been changed to protect the privacy of the interviewee.)

36. Information derived from interviews with former Third Ward residents Mario Carini and Libero Falso, Milwaukee, Wis., 2 and 4 March 2000 (Falso's name has been changed to protect the privacy of the interviewee); Milwaukee City Directories; and census data for Milwaukee.

37. Geib, "Italian Peddler," 109.

38. Mario Carini and Falso interviews, 2 March 2000.

39. Walter ("Blackie") Brocca, interview with author, Milwaukee, Wis., February 1993.

40. "The Spirit of Greenbush," a commemorative booklet published for the Greenbush Memorial public dedication ceremony, 14 October 2000, Madison, Wis.

41. For a discussion of the prominence of Italian women in the cigar industry, see Mormino and Pozzetta, *Immigrant World of Ybor City.*

42. Mario Carini and Falso interviews, 4 March 2000.

43. Tracy Poe, "Food, Culture, and Entrepreneurship among African Americans, Italians, and Swedes in Chicago" (Ph.D. diss., Harvard University, 1999), 155–56.

44. John Bodnar, *The Transplanted: A History of Immigrants in Urban America* (Bloomington: University of Indiana Press, 1985), 131.

45. Conzen, *Immigrant Milwaukee,* 114.

46. In addition, oral interviews reveal several more women who ran grocery stores but could not be located in either the city directories or the manuscript census.

47. Luciano Iorizzo, "Italian American Merchants as Seen in the R. G. Dunn Collection" (paper presented at the American Italian Historical Association Annual Conference, Washington, D.C., November 1992).

48. Information derived from Milwaukee City Directories and Wisconsin State Census for Milwaukee.

49. Ibid.

50. Ibid.

51. Balistreri interview.

52. Andrew Sanchirico, "Small Business and Social Mobility among Italian Americans," in *Italian Ethnics: Their Languages, Literature and Lives: Proceedings of the 20th Annual Conference of the American Italian Historical Association,* ed. Dominic Candeloro, Fred Gardaphe, and Paolo Giordano (Staten Island, N.Y.: American Italian Historical Association, 1990), 201–14.

53. Bartolone and Crivello interview.

54. A Black Hand operated in Milwaukee's Third Ward and engaged in extortion and petty racketeering during the early years of Italian settlement in Milwaukee.

55. Bartolone and Crivello interview.

56. Rampolla interview.

57. Ibid.

58. Kenneth Wilson and W. Allen Martin, "Ethnic Enclaves: A Comparison of the Cuban and Black Economies in Miami," *American Journal of Sociology* 88.1 (1982): 135–60.

59. Kenneth Wilson and Alejandro Portes, "Immigrant Enclaves: An Analysis of the Labor Market Experiences of Cubans in Miami," *American Journal of Sociology* 86.2 (1980): 295–319.

60. George E. Pozzetta, "Immigrants and Craft Arts: Scuola d'Industrie Italiane," in *The Italian Immigrant Woman in North America: Proceedings of the Tenth Annual Conference of the American Italian Historical Association,* ed. Betty Boyd Caroli, Robert Harney, and Lydio Tomasi (Toronto: Multicultural History Society of Ontario, 1978), 138–53.

61. Wendy Gamber, *The Female Economy: The Millinery and Dressmaking Trades, 1860–1930* (Urbana: University of Illinois Press, 1997), 30.

62. Susan Hay, ed., *From Paris to Providence: Fashion, Art, and the Tirocchi Dressmakers' Shop, 1915–1947* (Providence: Museum of Art, Rhode Island School of Design, 2000).

63. Vecchio, "Family Values and Culture," 40.

64. "Dressmaker, Italian Mentor Reunite," *Kenosha News,* 31 July 2000, C3.

65. Bodnar, *Transplanted,* 78.

66. Balistreri interview.

67. Ruby Stewart, "Women's Wages in Milwaukee," Bulletin 4, Milwaukee Bureau of Economy and Efficiency, June 1911, p. 10, Wisconsin State Historical Society, Milwaukee, Wis.

68. Ruiz, *Cannery Women, Cannery Lives,* 19.

69. Carini, *Milwaukee's Italians,* 53.

70. Wisconsin Bureau of Labor Statistics, 1900–01, Part VI, Women Employed in Factories, Archives, State Historical Society, Madison, Wis.

71. Mario Carini, interview with author, Milwaukee, Wis., February 2000.

72. Brocca interview.

73. Bartolone and Crivello interview.

74. LaPiana, *Italians in Milwaukee,* 11.

75. Ibid.

76. Rose Carini, interview with author, Milwaukee, Wis., 23 January 1991.

77. Mario Carini interview, February 2000.

78. LaPiana, *Italians in Milwaukee,* 11.

79. Willet, *Employment of Women,* 36.

80. Daniels, "No Place Like Home"; and Boris and Daniels, *Homework.*

81. Julia Kirk Blackwelder, *Women of the Depression: Caste and Culture in San Antonio, 1929–1939* (College Station: Texas A&M University Press, 1998), 93–102.

82. Interviews reveal large numbers of Sicilians whose parents and grandparents operated small-business establishments in Sicily.

Chapter 4: Female Professionals in the Immigrant Community

1. Application for a Certificate of Registration, Wisconsin Board of Medical Examiners, Midwife File, box 1, folder 16, number 260, State Board of Medical Examiners, Archives Division, Wisconsin State Historical Society, Madison, Wis. (hereafter Midwife File).

2. Italians, more than any other immigrant group, relied on midwives. In her 1906 sample of midwife deliveries in New York City, social worker Elisabeth Crowell found that of 1,029 births among Italian women, only 67 (7 percent) were reported by physicians and the remaining 962, or 93 percent, were reported by midwives. See Elisabeth Crowell, "The Midwives of New York," *Charities and the Commons* 17 (January 1907): 667–77. In 1917, Dr. Julius Levy reported that in Newark, N.J., "very few Italian mothers are delivered in hospitals, 88% are delivered by midwives." See Julius Levy, "The Maternal and Infant Mortality in Midwifery Practice in Newark, New Jersey," *American Journal of Obstetrics and Diseases of Women and Children* 77 (1918): 41–53.

3. Quoted by Charlotte G. Borst, "Wisconsin's Midwives as Working Women: Immigrant Midwives and the Limits of a Traditional Occupation, 1870–1920," *Journal of American Ethnic History* 8.2 (Spring 1989): 24–59.

4. Numbers compiled from the 1925 New York State Manuscript Census for Cortland, N.Y. Vincenza Fiorentini was the one practicing midwife serving the immigrant generation in Cortland.

5. See Charlotte Borst, *Catching Babies: The Professionalization of Childbirth, 1870–1920* (Cambridge: Harvard University Press, 1995).

6. Midwife registration records can be found in the Archives Division of the State Historical Society, Madison, Wis. In Milwaukee the Physicians Records on Midwifery are housed in the Archives of the Milwaukee Public Library.

7. Beth Rushing, "Turn-of-the-Century Midwifery Practice among North American Ethnic Women," in *Ethnic Women: A Multiple Status Reality*, ed. Vasilikie Demos and Marcia Texler Segal (Dix Hills, N.Y.: General Hall, 1994), 104–14.

8. Ibid., 104.

9. Helen Z. Papanikolas, "Magerou: The Greek Midwife," *Utah Historical Quarterly* 38.1 (1970): 50–60.

10. Buss, *La Partera*, 70.

11. Onnie Lee Logan, *Motherwit: An Alabama Midwife's Story* (New York: Dutton, 1991).

12. Judy Barrett Litoff, *American Midwives, 1860 to the Present* (Westport, Conn.: Greenwood, 1978), 27.

13. Nancy Schrom Dye, "Modern Obstetrics and Working-Class Women: The New York Midwifery Dispensary, 1890–1920," *Journal of Social History* 20 (Spring 1987): 548–64.

14. Cited by Rushing, "Midwifery Practice," 104–14.

15. Eugene R. Declerq, "The Nature and Style of Practice of Immigrant Midwives in Early Twentieth Century Massachusetts," *Journal of Social History* 10 (1985): 113–29.

16. Robert Foerster observed in 1919 that in the Italian neighborhoods of New York City "doctor and midwife might make a living while scarcely leaving the block." See Robert Foerster, *The Italian Emigration of Our Times* (New York: Arno, 1960), 382.

17. Statistics of Luisa Giordano's deliveries were compiled by examining all of the birth certificates during her years of practice. County Clerk's Office, Kenosha, Wis.

18. Milwaukee County Medical Society, Fee Bill, 1 May 1883, Milwaukee County Historical Society, Milwaukee, Wis.

19. Elizabeth Ewen, *Immigrant Women in the Land of Dollars: Life and Culture on the Lower East Side, 1880–1925* (New York: Monthly Review Press, 1985), 131.

20. Lee W. Thomas, "The Supervision of Midwives in New York City," *Monthly Bulletin, Department of Health, City of New York* 9 (May 1919): 117–20.

21. Charlotte Borst, "The Training and Practice of Midwives: A Wisconsin Study," *Bulletin of the History of Medicine* 62 (1988): 608–27.

22. Nancy Schrom Dye, "Mary Breckinridge, the Frontier Nursing Service, and the Introduction of Nurse-Midwifery in the United States," in *Women and Health in America,* ed. Judith Walzer Leavitt (Madison: University of Wisconsin Press, 1984), 327–43.

23. Quoted in Neal Devitt, "The Statistical Case for Elimination of the Midwife: Fact versus Prejudice, 1890–1935," *Women and Health* 4.1 (Spring 1979): 81–93.

24. Angela Danzi, "Old World Traits Obliterated: Immigrant Midwives and the Medicalization of Childbirth," in *Italian Ethnics: Their Languages, Literature, and Lives: Proceedings of the 20th Annual Conference of the American Italian Historical Association,* ed. Dominic Candeloro, Fred Gardaphe, and Paolo Giordano (Staten Island, N.Y.: American Italian Historical Association, 1990), 215–30.

25. Borst, "Training and Practice of Midwives," 620–26.

26. Physicians Records (midwifery), Milwaukee Public Library, Archives, Milwaukee, Wis.

27. Midwife File, box 1, folder 26, no. 25.

28. Josephine Cialdini (Luisa Giordano's godchild), interview with author, Kenosha, Wis., 11 November 1993.

29. Midwife File, box 1, folder 3.

30. Midwife File, box 1, folder 3.

31. Midwife File, box 1, folder 16.

32. *Milwaukee Sentinel,* 25 January 1976.

33. Midwife File, box 1, folder 17.

34. Quoted in Doris Weatherford, *Foreign and Female: Immigrant Women in America, 1840–1930* (New York: Facts on File, 1995), 31.

35. Devitt, "Elimination of the Midwife," 85.

36. Charlotte Borst, "Catching Babies: The Change from Midwife to Physician-Attended Childbirth in Wisconsin, 1870–1930" (Ph.D. diss., University of Wisconsin, Madison, 1989), 63.

37. Alessandro Cuzzi, *Manuale di ostetricia ad uso delle levatrici* (Milan: Francesco Vallardi, 1914).

38. Borst, "Catching Babies," 63.

39. See Barbara Melosh, *The Physician's Hand: Work Culture and Conflict in American Nursing* (Philadelphia: Temple University Press, 1982), 50.

40. Author's interviews with Louis Martino (brother of midwife Rosa Cesario), 9 November 1993; and Angelina Zonfrillo and Giuseppina Romanelli (daughters of Margherita Ciotti), 28 September 1993, Kenosha, Wis. (Zonfrillo's and Romanelli's names have been changed to protect the privacy of the interviewees.)

41. Health Department Physicians Register, 1882–1907, vol. 1, Archives of the Milwaukee Public Library.

42. Midwife File, box 1, folder 3.

43. Midwife File, box 1, folder 3, no. 363.

44. Borst, "Catching Babies," 194.

45. Borst, "Wisconsin's Midwives," 47.

46. New York City Clerk's Office, Birth Certificates (1904), Manhattan.

47. Judith Walzer Leavitt, *Brought to Bed: Childbearing in America, 1750–1950* (New York: Oxford University Press, 1986), 97.

48. Pietro di Donato, *Christ in Concrete* (reprinted New York: Signet, 1993), 39.

49. Angela Danzi, "Home Is Better: Childbirth and Continuity, New York City, 1920–1940" (paper presented at the American Italian Historical Association Conference, Washington, D.C., 1992).

50. Carolyn Pontillo, interview with author, Kenosha, Wis., 24 January 1994. Carolyn Pontillo reported that she selected Luisa Giordano as her midwife upon recommendation from her sister.

51. Nancy Triolo, "The Angelmakers: Fascist Pro-Natalism and the Normalization of Midwives in Sicily" (Ph.D. diss., University of California at Berkeley, 1989), 29.

52. Pontillo interview.

53. Rose Carini interview, 26 August 1992.

54. Crowell, "Midwives in New York," 672.

55. Pontillo interview; Zonfrillo and Romanelli interview.

56. Pontillo interview.

57. Zonfrillo and Romanelli interview.

58. Cialdini interview. Giordano rented a flat from Josephine Cialdini's parents. Growing up, Josephine spent much of her time in her godmother's flat, running errands for her and accompanying her to deliveries.

59. In her study of Italians in Greenwich Village during the 1920s, Carolyn Ware observed that "Italian women who sought to use contraceptives were driven to

acquire them secretly through the Italian midwives." See Caroline Ware, *Greenwich Village, 1920–1930* (New York: Harper and Row, 1965), 179.

60. Cialdini interview.

61. Triolo, "Angelmakers," 95.

62. Ibid., 95–98.

63. Pasqualine Pace, interview with author, Milwaukee, Wis., September 1992. (The name has been changed to protect the privacy of the interviewee.)

64. Martino interview; Zonfrillo and Romanelli interview.

65. Linda Gordon, *Woman's Body, Woman's Right: Birth Control in America* (New York: Penguin, 1990), 151.

66. Massimo Livi-Bacci, *L'immigrazione e l'assimilazione degli Italiani negli Stati Uniti* (Milan: Giuffre, 1961).

67. John Briggs, "Fertility and Cultural Change among Families in Italy and America," *American Historical Review* 91.5 (December 1986): 1129–45.

68. Verrico interview.

69. Quoted in Triolo, "Angelmakers," 114.

70. Ibid., 115.

71. Charlotte Gower-Chapman, *Milocca: A Sicilian Village* (Cambridge, Mass.: Schenkman, 1971), 116.

72. Maria La Bella and Ida Verrico, interviews with author, Santi Cosma e Damiano, Italy, April 2000.

73. Robert Sorci (grandson of Pasqua Cefalu), interview with author, Milwaukee, Wis., August 1993.

74. Martino interview.

75. "Obituary," *Milwaukee Sentinel,* 26 January 1976.

76. Regulation and Licensing, Medical Examining Board, Complaint and Revocation File, series 1873, box 1, Archives, State Historical Society of Wisconsin, Madison, Wis.; "Woman Accused in Death of Girl," *Milwaukee Sentinel,* 10 February 1937; "Midwife Gets 4 to 6 Years," *Milwaukee Sentinel,* 27 May 1937.

77. Martino, Cialdini, and Zonfrillo and Romanelli interviews.

78. ONMI, the Organization for the Protection of Mothers and Infants, was instituted by the Fascists in 1925. With nearly ten thousand centers nationwide, ONMI offered aid, information, and medical services to mothers in line with the pronatalist goals of the state. For more on this see Triolo, "Angelmakers."

Epilogue

1. Richard Whitmire, "The Young Italians Aren't Coming Home," *Binghamton Sunday Press,* 8 May 1977.

2. Zahavi, *Workers, Managers, and Welfare Capitalism,* 151–52.

3. George F. Johnson to George W. Johnson, February 1935. Writing to his son,

George F. admits that he would like to resume drawing a salary in April, if that would be acceptable to everyone. George F. Johnson Papers, Main Office, Endicott Johnson Corporation, Endicott, N.Y.

4. Maria Carmine Sepe, interview with author, Endicott, N.Y., May 1991. (The name has been changed to protect the privacy of the interviewee.)

5. Blackwelder, *Now Hiring,* 151.

6. Cohen, *Workshop to Office.*

7. Smith, *Family Connections,* 214.

8. Elsie DeGhera Falbo, interview with Lawrence Baldassaro, Milwaukee, Wis., 8 April 1991.

9. Tom Busalacchi, interview with author, Milwaukee, Wis., 3 March 1991.

10. Grace Gagliano Falbo, interview with Lawrence Baldassaro, Milwaukee, Wis., 5 April 1991.

11. Gaetanina Balistreri, interview with author, Milwaukee, Wis., 13 April 1991.

Index

130 · INDEX

tion growth, Milwaukee, 21; and proximity to homes, 42–43, 63, 80–81; regional variation in, 2, 3–4, 11–14; single women and, 35, 37, 58, 79; women's participation in, factors influencing, 4, 34–36, 43, 59, 62–64, 78–79; women's participation in, rates of, 2, 11, 30, 35–36, 63. *See also* agricultural labor; clerical work; factory workers; homework; Italy
Weaver, Helen, 37–38
Weber, Michael, 52
welfare capitalism: and childcare, 49–50; employee benefits under, 46, 47–48, 49, 115n87; housing under, 50–53; and Italian workers, 54–55; motivation for, 47, 48, 54, 55; and organized labor, 45, 54, 56; and working women, 4, 48–49. *See also* Endicott Johnson Corporation

West Allis, Wis., 21
wheat production, 20
wholesale trade, 29–30
Wickersham Commission, 71
Wisconsin, 20, 22, 62–63, 85, 89, 90. *See also* Milwaukee, Wis.
Wisconsin School of Midwifery, 85
women's employment, models of, 6
Wood, Dolores Bianco, 57

Yans, Virginia, 52, 59, 67
Ybor City, Fla., 3, 106n9
Yung, Judy, 66

Zahavi, Gerald, 45, 54
Zappi, Elda Gentili, 12
Zizzo, Vincenza, 72

Diane C. Vecchio is an associate professor of history and women's studies at Furman University in Greenville, South Carolina.

Statue of Liberty–Ellis Island Centennial Series